…And That's How the Rent Gets Paid
Billy and His Daddy

Jeff Weiss

Contact:
Blue Heron Book Works, LLC
610-653-6959
info@blueheronbookworks.com

ISBN-9781548450502
ISBN-10 1548450502

Blue Heron Book Works, LLC
Allentown, Pennsylvania 18104

www.blueheronbookworks.com

"My dear friend and classmate at Juilliard, Nancy Nichols turned me on to Jeff Weiss and East Village Experimental Theatre in the late 1960s. She was a member of a select group of actors working with Jeff. I had never seen such abandon, bravery, or limitless boundaries as I did watching Jeff act and digesting his brilliant plays, all directed by Riccardo Martinez. They were nights filled with ecstasy and transcendence. Lessons I'll treasure forever. Jeff Weiss is a brave, unsung American theatre genius."—*Patti LuPone*

An Introduction to Jeff Weiss' ....And That's How the Rent Gets Paid

What you have before you are extraordinary artifacts of a theatre created by Jeff Weiss and Carlos Ricardo Martinez. Together they produced a primal theatre, totally without pretension that told the truth about a world where self-interest and self-gratification were core values; values that drove people into the depths of a hell of unspeakable (and often very entertaining) depravity These texts came gloriously alive in performances performed by legions of actors dedicated to the truly democratic ethos created by Jeff and Carlos. On simple stages, sans scenic spectacle or contemporary performance technology (no computers, no microphones, no projections—just a piano, a few flashlights and perhaps a light switch for the blackouts) outrageous stories were performed punctuated by wonderful songs sung with great gusto by terrific singers.

The shows often went on for hours, sometimes for weeks. Jeff created mountains of text that actors memorized and performed with fearless spontaneity. Being in and around one of these productions was always a grand adventure imbued with true humanity and a sure theatrical instinct. Audiences in the lower east side of Manhattan or in Allentown, Pennsylvania were electrified by these plays. The texts can begin to give you the flavor of what went on at a Weiss/Martinez production, but like the best dramatic writing these plays really lived in the basements and lofts where the magic happened.

Taken together these plays are a monument to the relationship of Jeff and Carlos. It was a relationship that spanned over fifty years and it was a relationship that produced one of the most celebrated (numerous critical raves and a raft of Obie awards) bodies of creative work by any American theatre artist in the late 20th century. As Nancy Nichols has said:

> "To understand the love between Jeff and Richard
> and what they accomplished together is a matter
> of heart and soul. The day they met, Richard
> saved Jeff's life by turning off an unlit oven,
> unsealing taped up windows, flinging them open
> and letting in fresh air. Jeff showed his gratitude
> by opening his shuttered heart. He soon
> discovered he had a great reason to live –
> spending his life writing plays and making theater
> in collaboration with his friend Carlos Ricardo
> Martinez: Painter, Composer and Director
> extraordinaire.
>
> "Jeff was the electric light bulb. Richard, the
> power source. They completed each other like
> great teams do in their incongruous compatibility.

*If you had an ego and all actors do, Richard could
be a very difficult director. They'd wind up leaving
if they couldn't leave it at the door. For Richard,
theater, painting, any art form was all about
truth. Which is why his reputation suffered. He
never really minded. He left it at the door. "*

Enjoy these plays...revel in their dynamic energy, their
outrageous humor, but always remember that at their core, these
works make it very clear that there are consequences to our
actions and the real terror resides in ourselves.

Charles Richter, June 2017

NOTE FROM THE PUBLISHER

"Billy and His Daddy" is the second story line of *"...And That's How the Rent Gets Paid."* The other story lines are *"The Saga of Vicki Sheisskopf"* and *"The Death of Pinocchio"* which are each published separately. Our editors worked with Jeff Weiss to get the scenes his original story lines in linear order but linear order was not the original intent of this play and Mr. Weiss assures us it's not his intent now. The scenes in the three story lines are meant to be mixed up and intertwined at the pleasure of the director to create new emphasis and meaning.

Please note that *"...And That's How the Rent Gets Paid"* is a satire of the highest order with adult themes. The characters are intended to be played by adults.

Sex: A Love Letter

It was a small-town party. Every academic, writer, painter, actor within a twenty-mile radius and wearing unusual jewelry attended, schlepping hunks of cheese, liters of red and worn incantations of their latest achievements. It was hot and I was keeping company with a bottle of Patron, when a devilishly handsome man sporting a pink crocheted wig handed me a post card: a warning from AARP to check your bunghole regularly for disease. The post card had a picture of a healthy bunghole.

"How do I know what my bunghole looks like?!" he said, twisting around to show me the difficulty. "I can't follow AARP's guidelines!"

He clearly had a filthy sense of humor, but he made me laugh, my only excuse for giving him my card which he used to call me at 3 o'clock that morning and left a message. I didn't know about Richard, Jeff's lover yet, or that Richard was in the late stages of Parkinson, or that Jeff was enjoying a rare night away from care-giving and was still in a celebratory mood when he got home. I just knew I didn't need friends who called at 3 o'clock in the morning.

Still, after months of shopping my non-traditional musical around to local theater departments, I finally dropped in on Jeff, who I had since learned was a big deal along with Richard in the avant-garde theater world in 1960's-70's New York—Obies, Guggenheims, laudatory write-ups in the *New York Times*. I wanted his opinion. I needed it. I didn't trust the local poohbahs to respond to my non-rhyming sentiments.

It turns out Jeff and Richard lived three blocks from me in Jeff's ancestral home, where they moved when Richard's Parkinsons made it impossible to navigate New York. The entire first floor was jammed with Richard's prodigious art output, a piano, music scores, records, books, CDs, DVDs, VHS tapes, corks from a million wine bottles, a non-functioning bathroom, a taped-up refrigerator that had been sealed since his father died 20 years before and an inexplicably leaking ceiling.

"We should probably talk on the porch," he told me.

Here's the thing about Jeff: he understands the art of seduction. And isn't seduction just seeing what the other person needs and giving it to them? Much like art, really. An artist sees things as they are and mirrors that reality, maybe glitter thrown on, but recognizable truth.

So, he seduced me and we became friends. We had both been born in the Lehigh Valley and had bolted and lived our adult lives elsewhere, returning only when personal circumstances mandated. We were both outsiders in our hometown, in our own families, the result being we can't stop recreating our hometown, our families in our work.

Despite our friendship and my suspicion that genius resided in him—he is the only person who remembers everything I've ever told him—I had never read Jeff's plays or seen them performed. I asked for copies and he said they were in boxes in somewhere. The original scripts were never re-printed, never filmed, never even copyrighted. It was only when Richard began to deteriorate rapidly that Jeff felt some urgency to collectivize his and Richard's creative life. I'd started a publishing company and it was only natural that we decided Blue Heron Book Works should publish his and Richard's plays.

After we published Richard's *Art the Rat*, we decided to tackle Jeff's tour de force, *...And That's How the Rent Gets Paid*, three story lines written over years for various actors: *The Saga of Vicki Sheisskopf*, *Billy and His Daddy*, and *The Death of Pinocchio*.

Nothing can really prepare you for the raw uncensored humanity of these plays. First out was *The Saga of Vicki Sheisskopf*. There are scenes where Vicki is pimping out her own children and murdering those who would deter her — which makes sense, trust me, in context, but at the end of the play there is a cannibal scene that had me questioning everything that is good and holy. Still, it wasn't until I got to *Billy and His Daddy* that I worried about getting arrested for publishing Jeff's work. It opens with a scene where the young Billy is seducing his father and, yes, it is consummated. But the point is, I came to realize, that it was consummated physically but not emotionally. It wasn't until I finished reading the whole story line that I saw Billy for what he was: a boy using his sexuality — the only sure weapon in his arsenal — to win his father's love. That he rejects his father's brand of love at the end is Billy's redemption. "You were supposed to take care of me," he says to his dying father and the accusation goes far beyond any incestuous event. You aren't supposed to use your children for your own aggrandizement. Billy is screaming, "See me for who I am! Love me!" and the fellow outlier — me — knows exactly what he is demanding: something he can never get. Billy is talking for all artists and, frankly, most children.

Over the course of our friendship, I've met actors who said performing in Jeff' plays made them see what theater could be and decided them on an acting and writing career. For myself: Publishing *...And That's How the Rent Get Paid* shook me to the core of my creative existence and made me up my own game.

And so, without further ado, I present *Billy and His Daddy*.

Bathsheba Monk

SCENES

SCENE 1: DADDY & BILLY: THE PICNIC

SCENE 2: THE SPELLING BEE, RED BANK NEW JERSEY, PART ONE

SCENE 3: LESTER BATTERSALL GOES TO BANGKOK FOR THE FIRST TIME, ALONE.

SCENE 4: BILLY "BUNGHOLE' BATTERSALL, AS A TEENAGE BOY, TALKS LIFE, DEATH, WRESTLING AND TURKEY WITH HIS DAD, LESTER. RED BANK, NEW JERSEY. USA. ONE TWO THREE HIT IT. [SIC]

SCENE 5: AN EARLY PAGE FROM THE BOOK OF BILLY

SCENE 6: THE HAIRLESS HEINY... PART II... LESTER BATTERSALL, RED BANK, N.J. AND HIS ESCORT, ROVER, PREPARE TO HAVE A PARTY IN BANGKOK.

SCENE 7: SATURDAY MATINEE AT THE BATTERSALL FAMILY HOME. BILLY AND HIS DAD THROW A PARTY FOR THE WRESTLING TEAM FROM RED BANK HIGH.)

SCENE 8: THE MOMENT OF MORTAL TRUTH FOR DOCTOR PRATT. BILLY, THE HUSTLER, TAKES HIS FEE.

SCENE 9: LESTER BATTERSALL GOES SHOPPING. BELOW HOUSTON. NYC

SCENE 10: THREE MINUTES AFTER THE SLASHING, LES RETURNS TO HIS CAR AND BILLY'S

SCENE 11: WOK STORMS INTO HIS DRESSING ROOM, BILLY AFTER HIM.

SCENE 12: THE HAIRLESS HINEY, PART IV: LESTER GAMBOLS IN THE GARDEN OF SEXUAL DELIGHTS

SCENE 13: BLACKOUTS FROM THE HAIRLESS HINEY... BANGKOK

SCENE 14: BILLY RELEASES HIS FATHER FROM BONDAGE

SCENE 1: DADDY & BILLY: THE PICNIC

BILLY

Daddy,I'm home!

DADDY

Come-up, son. I gotta surprise!

BILLY

Should I take-off my pants?

DADDY

Do you think it would help?

BILLY

Couldn't hurt.

DADDY

Your right. We are in show-business.

BILLY

I'm stuffed for the picnic. Take a whiff.

(BILLY thrusts his fat dick in his father's
face)

DADDY

Stop! You'll knock-out my caps again!

BILLY

I'm so excited, down in my balls where it matters, pop.

DADDY

... and a nice long talk with your father.

BILLY

Is he coming?

DADDY

Billy!

BILLY

Yessir.

DADDY

I'm your father.

10

                                  BILLY
Sure you are, daddy. (a pause) I jus' forgot.

                                  DADDY
We've never had a picnic, have we, Billy?

                                  BILLY
I guess not. (a pause) What is a picnic, papa?

                                  DADDY
A picnic's when you go out with the folks to the woods and fuck around in the trees and bushes.

                                  BILLY
Outside??!

                                  DADDY
Ah-huh.

                                  BILLY
We're gonna wrestle outside, daddy?

                                  DADDY
Yes, Billy.

                                  BILLY
We always wrestle in the playroom, the garage...

                                  DADDY
Or here in the attic, yes.

                                  BILLY
We gonna take our mat...won't we?

                                  DADDY
Why should we?

                                  BILLY
Cause I don't think I could do it in the grass with you.

                                  DADDY
On the bare ground, hard & ungiving.

                                  BILLY
What about the other people?

                                  DADDY
In the woods only those who want to watch will.

BILLY

Let's wrestle here, okay? Then we can go to the woods and fuck in the trees.

DADDY

We can do that too...after.

BILLY

I can't stay hard with people watching. I don't get-off outside.

DADDY

You can seven straight in two hours last Saturday afternoon, for God's sake...

BILLY

In the garage, not the woods.

DADDY

Look, Billy. Young guys from the country-club, college=boys on summer vacation, wander into the woods after work-outs. Hard. Hot. Pumped. Young men with muscles and a mission!

BILLY

Could I kill one?

DADDY

Sure. Think you can? Some of these boys are brutes.

BILLY

I can take the biggest in the pack and break his back...

DADDY

On acid, maybe. You could never do one straight....

BILLY

Hell, c'mon pop...I got so much acid in me I can't <u>think</u> straight! Half the time I wonder who you are. Gmme a break. You can work me up a frenzy daddy, you know you can. Throw me on the toughest stud you got...Shit, I'll bust his legs. I'll shove my cock so far down his throat he'll choke to death!

DADDY

Stop!

BILLY

Sure, pop.

DADDY

Step on the mat with me.

BILLY

Love to, daddy.

DADDY

You know what that does to me, don't you, when you do that?

BILLY

Do what, papa?

DADDY

When you show me how your gonna kill young guys....

BILLY

Nice cuts and too curious for their own good.

DADDY

Makes me hot...nostalgic...

BILLY

You did some guys in the woods with grandpa, right?

DADDY

(somewhat sheepishly)
Three. (holds-up four fingers.)

BILLY
That's four, pop.

DADDY

For the one that got away. (very moved by the memory & his finger)

BILLY
(equally moved)

Oh, daddy, daddy, daddy.

DADDY

Yes, Bill?

BILLY

I love when you get romantic like this....

DADDY

Memories are made of fingers such as these. (looks at his stranglers hands)

BILLY

That's when the sex gets really good....

DADDY

When daddy remembers....

BILLY
When we wrestle for the biggest prize of all....

DADDY
The present.

BILLY
Where time stands still.

DADDY
And anyone we want to kill, we can.

BILLY
Let me pin you pop and make you come.

DADDY
What if you come first?

BILLY
I might.

DADDY
Then I'll have to kiss your back and chew your hair while I fuck you...

BILLY
In that case, I will.

DADDY
Will what?

BILLY
Come first.

DADDY
Good for you. I raised my son to be a gentleman.

BILLY
For you, daddy, this butt is always open for business.

DADDY
Don't twist the tigers' dinghy, Billy. You're too hot...too hard for any man to handle.

BILLY
You can handle me.

DADDY
I can molest you.

BILLY

Molest me, then. Get me in a full-nelson, sport. I'll make you hard with my tight buns... Your peter's gonna pop right outta your pants when my ass gets working on it. Trust me.

DADDY

(Snaps into fantasy)
How long you been in prison, kid?

BILLY

Two weeks. You?

DADDY

Twenty years.

BILLY

An old con's cock is the sweetest meat in the clink. (pause) Or so I've been told.

DADDY

By whom?

BILLY

Other old cons like you.

DADDY

They lied. If chewing on an amputated leg is up your alley, I got just the cock for you...... You want sweet meat, see a butcher or blow yourself....

BILLY

I can. Wanna see?

DADDY

Back off a bit, okay. Never had me a boy so young and green and sweet like you come on to me like this before. I like you.

BILLY

You'll have to fight me to fuck me......

DADDY

That's okay.... I beat up all my boys before I fuck em.

BILLY

Ever meet a boy you couldn't beat?

DADDY

Not in twenty years.

BILLY

How come? You must have had a lotta fights with young guys... never once got
beat?

DADDY

If you're strong and fight dirty, you can fuck any boy you want.

BILLY

Teach me to fight dirty, okay? Show me how to win!!

DADDY

I'm into boys who need instruction.

BILLY

Instruct me. I'm stupid and strong. Try me.

DADDY

Let's say you got me in a head-lock.

BILLY

"You got me in a head-lock." That was easy. I'm no dumby.

DADDY

Yes you are! I said, put me in a head-lock.

BILLY

Like this? (gets DADDY awkwardly in a head-lock) How am I doing?

DADDY

You're breaking my neck.

BILLY

That's the point, no?

DADDY

This is NOT a debate.

Daddy does something behind BILLY's
back. BILLY screams, releases his father
and hops around the attic in great pain,
holding his butt with both hands.

BILLY

AH! OWWWW! OH, SHIT! WHOA, BILLY! THAT"S NOT FAIR!

Billy's legs are wobbly.

DADDY

What's fair in love and foreplay?

                         BILLY
You ripped the hair out of my ass, you fuck!

                         DADDY
Watch your language!

                         BILLY
Frankly, at a time like this, there are not words enough at hand, to pick and
choose.

                         DADDY
Nice turn of phrase. I'm not impressed.

                         BILLY
I read a lot.

                         DADDY
Quality paperbacks?

                         BILLY
Birthday cards. (remembers his throbbing ass) Ouch! You fight dirty!

                         DADDY
This dance we do is more apache than minuet.

                         BILLY
Now who's talking fancy, you fuck! You can bust a full-nelson, so what? I can
wrap my legs around you so tight, pops, squeeze you so hard, you'll spit-up your
lunch. How bout it, guy?? Wanna see?

                         DADDY
No need to consult my muse on that one, boy. Let's do it!

                                        THEY GRAPPLE. DADDY gets his leg
                                        behind BILLY's leg, yanks it out from under
                                        his son, and sends BILLY backward onto
                                        the mat. DADDY forces BILLY's arms to
                                        the mat. BILLY snaps his legs hard around
                                        his father. The father rears back and rams
                                        his fist into BILLY's groin.

                         BILLY
AW! OH! OWWWWW!

                                        BILLY's legs go dead and he curls up in the
                                        fetal position, cupping his wounded dick &
                                        balls in his hands, as DADDY rises to his
                                        feet and stands over his son.

DADDY

See how we do things in this man's army, kid?

BILLY

Oh, man! You shouldn't punch a boy in the cock that way! Might hurt him.
SHIT! You fuck-up my business like this, ow. How could you do that to your
son???!!

DADDY

You were the one brought this on, not me!

BILLY

Why can't you let me win once in awhile? Why do you always hurt me, pop?

DADDY

Get up. Face me.

BILLY

I can't. My cock hurts.

DADDY

Stand. Fight.

                        BILLY rises painfully, one hand on his cock
                        and balls, the other on his sore butt.

DADDY

BEAR HUG ME.

BILLY

I can't.

DADDY

Sure you can. How you gonna kill me some big husky college boy in the woods,
if you can't stand-up to your dear old dad? Crush me, Billy. See if you can!

                                     BILLY tries. Fails.

DADDY

Why waste time. This is how you crush a boy. Fast. No frills.

BILLY

Daddy! Stop! Let go! Daddy!

                        DADDY releases Billy, who drops to the
                        mat like a stone. BILLY, on his backs,
                        resting on his elbows, looks up at his father,
                        his face suffused with romantic avidity.

BILLY

Bury me, Daddy. Make me cum. Love me. Crush me. Do me!

His daddy does him. BILLY cums, thrashing under his father, like a young colt, as he does so. When BILLY calms, DADDY speaks.

DADDY

Shh. Daddy. Shh.

BILLY

Do you love me?

DADDY

Who wouldn't?

BILLY

Do you think about me all the time, cause I do you, all the time.

DADDY

I'd have to say you dominate my thoughts, that's true.

BILLY

And you dominate my body, that's a fact.

DADDY

I'm your father.

BILLY

I can't come with anyone else but you pop. Believe me, I've tried plenty.

DADDY

And you mustn't come with anyone else but me! Let me explain: We only get-off with each other...we stay clean. Nothing foreign to muck up the works, spoil our insides...Pristine.

BILLY

What's "pristine," pop?

DADDY

Ah, unsullied.

BILLY

What's "unsullied," daddy?

DADDY

Ah, ah, undefiled!

                                BILLY
Oh. (a pause) What's "undefiled???"

                                DADDY
CLEAN! BIOLOGICALLY & GENETICALLY SOUND! The blood stays in
the lab where it belongs.

                                BILLY
The lab?

                                DADDY
THE FAMILY, THEN! One small racial unit against the WORLD. The safest
sex. HOW DO YOU UNDERSTAND WHAT I MEAN BY PRISTINE????
YOU SEXY, RIPPED, LITTLE BOHUNK... COMMERE. BITE MY ARMS.

                            BILLY does.

                                BILLY
Oh, when you talk like this...treat me rough, then love me tender. It's
so...so...oh, what's the word?

                                DADDY
Pristine.

                                BILLY
Yeah. Pristine. Unsullied.

                                DADDY
Unsullied.

                                BILLY
Unsullied.

                                DADDY
And the biggest word of all, Billy?

                                BILLY
Clean, daddy.

                                DADDY
Clean, yes, and white.

                                BILLY
Like a brand new Kitchen sink.

                                DADDY
Nothing worn at all.

                                    BILLY
Everything fresh...

                                    DADDY
Spic & Span.

                                    BILLY
White & clean, like me and you, daddy.

                                    DADDY
Newfallen snow.

                                    BILLY
High-gloss enamel.

                                    DADDY
The wicker in the summer-house.

                                    BILLY
A baby's freshly powdered bottom.

                                    DADDY
Your stomach in winter's midst. Hard white tummy against freshly-laundered
shirts...

                                    BILLY
In the master bedroom...

                                    DADDY
The master, yes.

                                    BILLY
A boy on his belly bites a white pillow, his hard butt in the air...

                                    DADDY
So white.

                                    BILLY
So clean... like you always told me pop....

                                    DADDY
What's that, son?

                                    BILLY
Fresh blood looks great on clean white sheets.

                                    DADDY
I'm still hard.

BILLY

You didn't come?

DADDY

I was distracted, the picnic....

BILLY

I did. (digs a handful out from his shorts) Look!

DADDY

Whew! That's quite a pile of sperm you got there, son.

BILLY

Wanna taste?

DADDY

Sure. Why not? (dips his finger in BILLY's cupped hand and sucks his finger)
Hm. That's good. Here. Try some yourself.

(Dips his finger, offers to BILLY)

BILLY

I don't know. Tastes a little sour to me, no?

DADDY

What do you mean, "sour?" Let me see here... (dips again)... A trifle acidic,
maybe, not sour...musky, with a hint of mint....

BILLY

We suck lemons at wrestling practice...

DADDY

That's it, then... switch to a sports-drink or good old-fashioned H2O, I think
you'll find that sperm of yours will sweeten-up overnight.

BILLY

I want my cum to be sweet and clean, daddy. Don't you?

DADDY

I certainly do. And if it's not, trust me to be the first to tell you.: "Son, your cum
tastes funny...."

BILLY

And I'll be just as honest with you on your loads, dad, I promise.

DADDY

This way we can maintain "quality control" with no problems.

                              BILLY
And <u>never</u> taste like shit to each other. <u>Ever</u>!

                              DADDY
Good! On that elegant note, let's go to the woods...

                              BILLY
And kill me a college-boy.

                              DADDY
I love you so much, Billy, so much. You understand me. What turns me on.
We're an orchestra... of two. And we never kiss & tell.

                              BILLY
Kiss me, Daddy. (Daddy does) You won't tell, will you, pop.

                              DADDY
<u>I'll</u> never tell.

                              BILLY
My lips are sealed.

                              DADDY
To the edge of the grave... and beyond.

                              BILLY
Forever. Now <u>that's</u> what I call romance.

                              DADDY
BLACKOUT.

SCENE 2: THE SPELLING BEE, RED BANK NEW JERSEY, PART ONE

                                LESTER
Ruth?

                                RUTH
                                (off stage)
Yes, Les.

                                LESTER
Ask Billy to step into the den when he gets home, will ya?

                                RUTH
I will. Should I wear the white pants-suit or the organdy tutu with the parasol?

                                LESTER
Ahh... tutu.

                                RUTH
Great I love tutu.

                                Lester removes a strip of acid dots from his
                                wallet, pops the sheet into his mouth and
                                begins to chew.

                                LESTER
Me, too.

                                BILLY
                                (off stage)
Mom. I'm home.

                                LESTER
I'm peeling. Your Daddy. The den.

                                BILLY
Gotta shower first, mom. B.O.

                                LESTER
Your father loves B.O., Billy. He wants you.

                                BILLY
Okay.

                                Billy enters den, all hot & sweaty.

                    LESTER
Freeze.

                              Billy does.

                    BILLY
May I?

                    LESTER
You may. (Billy does) You're all hot & sweaty.

                    BILLY
I'm nervous, pop. Big day.

                    LESTER
Very big. I'm so proud of you, Billy.

                    BILLY
Thanks. And I'm so proud you're proud of me, pop.

                    LESTER
And I'm so proud you're proud that I'm proud of you.

                    BILLY
Yeah, dad. And you know what the bestest part of all this is?

                    LESTER
Tell me. What?

                    BILLY
I'm more proud you're proud that I'm proud you're proud...

                    LESTER
CUT THAT OUT!

                    BILLY
I want to make you happy.

                    LESTER
You do. I look at you, I'm happy.

                    BILLY
I'm so proud you're happy.

                    LESTER
And I'm so happy you're proud. Plus, I've just about had it with pride and
happiness, I could kutz. [pronounced, "Cuts"]

BILLY

Me, too.

LESTER

You're the only Battersall in all the years the Red Bank Spelling Bee has been, to make the finals. Wow.

BILLY

Wow. I can't believe my good fortune.

LESTER

All in the genes, Billy Boy. You're gonna go out there this afternoon and win the Bee.

BILLY

I'm gonna give it my best, coach.

LESTER

All you've got and then some, Billy. How wiil you handle that slippery little Jap from Emmaus High next Saturday?

BILLY

Bust a couple of his ribs before I pin him.

LESTER

First year. No losses. Coach Sawicky got himself a pearl beyond price when he chose you for the Junior Squad, Billy. Now the Spelling Bee. Was almost worth the whole shebang, wasn't it.

BILLY

The whole magilla and then some, pop.

LESTER

Put your money on Billy Battersall.

BILLY

All my bones are healed. Feel stronger than ever. Thin. Strong.

LESTER

Like a reed that bends, Billy, and won't be broken.

BILLY

The acid helps, Pop...

LESTER

Good. I'm glad you like it. How many tabs have you taken today, son?

                              BILLY
Two and a half.

                             LESTER
Good. You'll be "up" like an airship for the Bee... all spit and polish... so slender
and clean... genetically advanced, mind and body, the perfect union.

                              BILLY
We can't really lose, can we?

                             LESTER
Not a chance.

                              BILLY
How many for you, dad? For the Bee.

                             LESTER
What?

                              BILLY
How many tabs for you?

                             LESTER
Been chewing a sheet for the last ten minutes.

                              BILLY
Whew! That's... what? 72 tabs?

                             LESTER
Hmm. That's right. I'm running this Spelling Bee, Billy, and I don't know about
anybody else... I'm determined to have a good time. I don't spend the major part
of each day hallucinating, that day's a total loss to me. Not quite right. Out of
whack with my genetic imperatives.

                         A pause. A clock ticking.

                              BILLY
Dad?

                             LESTER
Yes, Billy.

                              BILLY
I'm gonna take a shower.

                             LESTER
Good idea. HOT. Sweaty.

                         Lester advances on his son.

                            BILLY
B.O.

                    His dad smells his son's armpits.

                    LESTER
Someone should rub your back.

                    BILLY
Would you scrub my back, daddy?

                    LESTER
In a New York minute.

                    BILLY
Oh, boy o boy o boy. Now I'm getting all excited, tore-up in my balls... the sac
is so full , pop... my bags are packed... I'm coming, Jesus... Hold me, daddy.
Carry me to the toilet. Shower me. Scrub me...

                    LESTER
(to the audience)
To you all, I humbly submit: This is why fathers want sons.

                    Lester carries his son to the toilet.

Mr. Sandman's song [sic]

BLACKOUT

SCENE 3: LESTER BATTERSALL GOES TO BANGKOK FOR THE FIRST TIME, ALONE.

                              LESTER
Who's there?

                              VOICE
Reggie?

                              LESTER
Reggie who?

                              VOICE
Reggie Poon Tang from the Yellow Peril Escort Service.

                              LESTER
Come in. The door's open.

                                        A lean dark Asian man in white cut-
                                        off jeans, white tank-top, sneakers
                                        without sox, a straw hat on his head,
                                        enters. He carries a book bag.

                              REGGIE
Mr. Battersall?

                              LESTER
Lester Battersall, but you can call me "sir."

                              REGGIE
Yes, sir. I am Reggie your guide to the late-nite pleasures of Old Bang-kok. You
can call me anything you like.

                              LESTER
Because I pay you... or does submitting turn you on?

                              REGGIE
I'll admit to getting horny when a customer calls me "Rover." I don't much care
for "pig" or "slut."

                              LESTER
Who can blame you?

                                        There is a pause while the two men
                                        look at each other, with some
                                        intensity... in the damp heat of the
                                        night.

                          LESTER
What are you looking at?

                          REGGIE
You. Who else?

                          LESTER
Do you like what you see?

                          REGGIE
You're more and less than I expected.

                          LESTER
Were you waiting for me?

                          REGGIE
Russell Moffler had this room last week.

                          LESTER
How is the old crock of shit?

                          REGGIE
Bad kidney.

                          LESTER
Still?

                          REGGIE
Tight ass.

                          LESTER
You took a shot at Russell's one good feature, bully for you.

                          REGGIE
I can't resist a tight old butt! Russell told me about you.

                          LESTER
What did he tell you?

                          REGGIE
Said you were wired. Wild. Hot.

                          LESTER
Thank him for me will you when you see him.... if he lives?

                          REGGIE
I will. And Billy. He told me about Billy.

LESTER

Billy. My perfect boy. I'm not surprised. All the guys from Boyz Love, Inc.
want Billy. They know he's mine.

REGGIE

I hear when guys take you or Billy on, they come away with broken bones and
ruptured rectums, if they come away at all.

LESTER

Ever wrestled, Reggie?

REGGIE

In high school.

LESTER

Were you good?

REGGIE

I was fast.

LESTER

Were you strong?

REGGIE

I was light.

LESTER

ARE YOU STRONG?!

REGGIE

My legs are very strong.

LESTER

I see. Have you ever wrestled in a naked frenzy with a 12-year-old boy and
broke his back?

REGGIE

Not that I recall.

LESTER

I will. Tonight.

REGGIE

I'd like to see that.

LESTER

I'll bet. You're lethal, Tang. I like you. (pause) This sex club...

REGGIE

The Hairless Hiney.... yes?

LESTER

Is it... safe?

REGGIE

Very kinky and discrete. Protected. Out back the Suey Canal runs down to the Sea of Wapiti. "Kiss em and kill em." You read the brochure.

LESTER

I want to be safe, Poon. Gotta business back in Red Bank, New Jersey. Sporting goods. A wife. Community Leader. Billy. The Garage. The Play Room. The Tool Shed. I want no diplomats' sons on a tear. No Japs. Expendable young Thai boys who'll never be missed.

REGGIE

As we speak, sir, some of those boys are dead already.

LESTER

(lets out a huge sigh)
I think I'm going to like Bangkok, Rover.

REGGIE

(without much enthusiasm)
woof woof. Why did you leave your son at home?

LESTER

Next year for his sixteenth birthday. Call me the advance guard. Gotta check out the territory, sniff out the spots where havoc holds the day.

REGGIE

That's a very lovely way to put it, sir.

LESTER

Wrote poetry in high school. Had Billy when I was 40. For years I knocked around the Jersey Shore. Never came close to catching me, Jersey cops. Killed one out by Cape May. Hot. Big cock. Dead cock!

REGGIE

If it's not too personal, sir, how many guys do you think you've...

LESTER

Dozens. (pause) Sure. Dozens. Many dozens.

REGGIE

And Billy?

LESTER

Together, a couple of thousand pounds of beef have gone through the grinder of our passions, Reggie. What he's done on his own, I can't say. I don't meddle in my son's personal affairs. I'm a Scientologist.

REGGIE

Whew! I never had a client quite like you.

LESTER

On balance, Id say you've been lucky, until now.

REGGIE

(giggling boyishly,
with some
nervousness)

You won't kill me, will you?

LESTER

Not you. I can use you. You're my guide. Wanna see a picture of Billy?

REGGIE

Love to.

Lester fishes a photo, laminated, out of his butt, sprays it with disinfectant, sniffs it, seems satisfied and proudly presents Billy's picture to Reggie.

Whoa, what a beautiful white body.

LESTER

Damn right he's white!

REGGIE

Hm. Nice fat weiner.

LESTER

That's one husky slab of meat... trust me.

REGGIE

His buns look good enough to eat.

LESTER

I know. Chew on them every chance I get.

REGGIE

Got a set of legs I could kiss all night.

LESTER

Totally depilitoried.

REGGIE

Smooth.

LESTER

Not one hair on his perfect body.

REGGIE

Wow! I'd pay you anything you'd ask, for one hour on a mat with Billy, Mr. Battersall.

LESTER

Show me a good time, I'll invite you to his 16th birthday party.

REGGIE

Would you? I'd love that.

LESTER

You're about his size. Lean. Wiry. Solid. I'll watch, of course.

REGGIE

I'd be disappointed if you didn't.

LESTER

Probably jump on the two of you without warning.

REGGIE

I'd like that.

LESTER

You guys could gang up on me. Beat me. Pin me. Fuck me.

REGGIE

I can do that.

LESTER

You can, but will you?

REGGIE

I can try. I'm stronger than you think.

LESTER

Could I interest you in a tab of acid?

REGGIE

I'll take two if you're sharing.

34

LESTER

Good. Here.

       (They guzzle
       tabs of acid,
       washed
       down with
       Southern
       Comfort.)

Ooo whee! Hurry on down to my house, baby, there ain't nobody home but me.

REGGIE

Finally. A customer with class.

LESTER

Thanks, Rover.

REGGIE

Woof, woof.

LESTER

I covet your hard, brown body and twisted mind.

REGGIE

Thank you, sir. Oh, by the way, what's this, here? (refers to Billy's photo)

LESTER

Where?

REGGIE

On the floor there, next to Billy's foot.

LESTER

Oh. A stomach. (a pause)

REGGIE
(giggles nervously)

Ooooooo. Any one I know?

LESTER

That's Brewster Wilson's stomach.

REGGIE

Nice abs.

LESTER

Was on the wrestling team with Billy at Red Bank High.

REGGIE

What did you do with the rest of him?

LESTER

We kept one sturdy leg and the washboard abdominals... the remains... (an awful pause). I'd rather not say.

REGGIE

One question, sir.

LESTER

Yes?

REGGIE

Why do you keep Billy's picture up your ass?

LESTER

What can I tell you? I miss him like the dickens. Besides, I promised. And he'll wear my underwear until I get home. I'm a sentimental kind of guy. So's Billy. We share everything. Toothbrush. Semen. Enemas. Popcorn.

REGGIE

Wish I had a daddy like you.

LESTER

Wanna be my best boy for a night?

REGGIE

Be your son?

LESTER

Why not? You're like him in all the ways that make me hot.

REGGIE

I got myself a boner, Mr. Battersall.

LESTER

You're not alone. Have a bit of a stiffy myself. Call me "Sir." Look! Let's pretend it's next year. I've brought you with me for your 16th birthday. To Bangkok. Everything's in order... no?!

REGGIE

Ready for Freddy, sir.

LESTER

Haven't shot our loads in about three weeks.

REGGIE

My dick's already sore.

LESTER

You'll wear his shorts, his sneakers and his socks. His jock-strap and his tee-shirt. And...(with a flourish, from a shopping bag) A short blonde wig.

REGGIE

This wacko-shit is right up my alley, sir. (puts the wig on) Wanna wrestle, daddy?

LESTER

Must not waste your thick teenage seed on me, Billy. Tonite's your birthday. Save that load for your first live fuck.

REGGIE

Can I pick my own ass?

LESTER

You'e sixteen, Billy. Pick him. Pummel him. Fuck him. Kill him. Say, where you from?

REGGIE
Modesto, California.

LESTER

You're an American?

REGGIE

Ah-huh. Working my way through college.

LESTER

Your folks alive?

REGGIE

My dad. Taps the vats for Gallo.

LESTER

A college boy?

REGGIE

I know my P's and Q's. Look, Mr. Battersall. Let me level with you.

LESTER

I like a guy what's on the level.

REGGIE

I sucked a lot of cock in San Francisco. Had sex with a pig in Sweden. Couple of Kung Fu Pictures in Hong Kong for Run Run Shaw. Done strip shows as Malo, The Sexual Outlaw. Probed the glory holes of Old Manhattan and ate a Bishop's dick. I shot a dozen eggs out of my ass at the Blind Adonis, the hottest act they ever booked. I'm not about to say I've lived a blameless life, so far, far from it... I've killed before and will again... Never like this! Hey! I blew Salvador Dali, and didn't get sick. I'm no prince. But you! You're closer to Heaven than any Hell I could wish for. You're really sick, Mr. Battersall. You're one sick old fuck... sir.

(A long pause)

                              LESTER
Let's hit the Hairless Hiney with a pair of ten-inch pricks and have a party.

                              REGGIE
You're my daddy, man. You're my daddy.

                              LESTER
Rover?

                              REGGIE
Woof woof.

                              LESTER
You got the wig on backwards.

                              REGGIE
                              (straightens wig)
Gotcha, daddy.

They exit. We hear the ticking of a clock in the empty room for several beats.

BLACKOUT

SCENE 4: BILLY "BUNGHOLE' BATTERSALL, AS A TEENAGE BOY, TALKS LIFE, DEATH, WRESTLING AND TURKEY WITH HIS DAD, LESTER. RED BANK, NEW JERSEY. USA. ONE TWO THREE HIT IT.

(Billy knocks on door.)

LESTER

Come in, son.

BILLY enters in tight sweat pants and tight tank-top. Barefoot. Very sweaty.

BILLY

I ran all the way home when I heard you wanted me.

LESTER

Billy. Give a hug.

(They come together like gladiators, bear-hugging each other. The father wins.)

LESTER

That was good.

BILLY

Yes. Was. You're a hard man, daddy. Tough. How was Thailand?

LESTER

Same old shit. The boys were hot. Are you stiff?

BILLY

I am.

LESTER

Good. I spoke to Sawicky.

BILLY

He told you.

LESTER

Your Coach is candid. Who's Brewster Willlson?

BILLY

New boy on the team. Came over from Phillipsburg.

LESTER

Sawicky told me he beat you.

BILLY

I was sick.

LESTER

The flu?

BILLY

The enemas.

LESTER

First thing your grandmother taught me about the body, Billy: keep the colon clean.

BILLY

Yeah, but between the ammonia douches, diuretics, enemas and Hi-Pro Fruit Bars... I was too thin, Dad.

LESTER

You must be clean, son, inside & out, to fight this good fight. For fathers everywhere...

BILLY

Forever.

LESTER

My peer group thanks you.

BILLY

I'm clean, papa, you've smelled my ass often enough to know.

LESTER

Never intentionally. On some holds I get a whiff... (he sniffs) ahh Amazon Rain Forest.

BILLY

I couldn't take him. He was too thick. In the legs.

LESTER

Sawicky says your takedowns were fine. Your reversals were sloppy.

BILLY

He was all over me, dad. He was a tough boy, pop. Honest.

LESTER

Could he take your father?

BILLY

No one can take my father.

LESTER

I'd like to meet this Brewster Willson.

BILLY

Here, in the garage?

LESTER

About 2. Saturday. Regular time. When your mother's at group.

BILLY

I don't know, pop. His dad's a cop.

LESTER

We'll take it slow and easy.

BILLY

Could I ask a favor?

LESTER

Sure.

BILLY

Let me oil him.

LESTER

I do the oiling.

BILLY

I'd like to do his legs, if that's okay with you.

LESTER

We can share. Take whichever leg you want.

BILLY

Let's not go all the way with this one, okay?

LESTER

Don't be silly, Billy. These husky Jersey boys come & go. Like the wind. At the Shore.

BILLY

Brewster's beautiful.

LESTER

Tell me how beautiful.

BILLY

The minute I saw him, I wanted him. Perfect. Clean. My size. More heavily
muscled. With these great cuts in his thighs. Swollen calves. Vascular. The way
you like 'em, pop.

LESTER

And he destroyed you.

BILLY

Submission. Between the legs.

LESTER

Sawicky told me.

BILLY

I'm sorry.

LESTER

This boy can beat you for a berth on the squad. How does it feel to lose to
another boy?

BILLY

Losing to a man I'm used to. This is the first boy ever made me give,

LESTER

I want him.

BILLY

I'll bring him.

LESTER

By hook or by crook!?

BILLY

Any way that works. If I must drag him by the hair, I will.

LESTER

Good. So... Saturday we'll have our first three-way since... I can't remember.

BILLY

You're still in Bangkok. The week before your trip. That little Maltese guy from
the garage...

LESTER

Hard little butt. I bit it.

                              BILLY
The blood ran down the back of his legs.

                              LESTER
You strangled him with your thighs.

                              BILLY
You ruptured him with the handle of a mop.

                              LESTER
Hey. You jumped on his stomach till he spit up his lunch.

                              BILLY
Acid drives me nuts, dad. I told you. From before.

                              LESTER
Couldn't have weighed more 'n 120 pounds. Took him twenty minutes to die.

                    (A DEAD AWFUL PAUSE)

                              BILLY
                    (speaks suddenly)
That big Hungarian boy went in 6. Flat.

                              LESTER
                    (unbelieving)
Is that right?

                              BILLY
I timed it. You took him on the first fall. He rallied to gain the second. You
broke his back to take the match.

                              LESTER
HIs name? Do you remember his name?

                              TOGETHER
                    (with serene pleasure)
Vassily.

                              LESTER
Great back.

                              BILLY
Yeah. Vassily. Best dead ass I ever fucked, pop. Thanks to you.

                              LESTER
Which brings me to the second topic on our agenda for this weekend.

BILLY

Yes, dad.

LESTER

I been pretty easy on you since you joined the Team, haven't I?

BILLY

I'm grateful for the break.

LESTER

Your average is up, I'm pleased to note. And, except for this unfortunate tumble with Brewster Willson, the only undefeated wrestler at Red Bank High.

BILLY

Want you to be proud of me, pop. I love you... so... much...

LESTER

Let's not get sappy. Okay? Let's be men about this.

BILLY

Sometimes I wish we could, some Saturday afternoon, just lay down on the mat and... cuddle... nice sexy massage, a nap, maybe rub our dicks together till we cum... you know, slow & easy.

LESTER

That's too... too...

BILLY

Romantic?

LESTER

Nelly. The sex that matters between a man and his son starts in combat, ends in rape & violation. That's the world.

BILLY

But, daddy... you hurt me so.

LESTER

Your ass is clean. No lesions. At least there were none last time I looked.

BILLY

Dad! Stop! I've trained my butt to take a pop from you, Daddy. That's not what bugs me. You bite. Too hard. You squeeze me too hard.

LESTER

Not lately. I backed off.

BILLY

You don't want Sawicky to see the teeth marks, the welts, and bruises...

                              LESTER
That. And... other things.

                              BILLY
Oh, daddy, please, I want you to love me, not hurt me. You never kiss me on the
lips. You crush my cock in your hand till I scream. Why not lick me? Why not?

                              LESTER
Let women lick cock. They're used to that. We wrestle. I whip you. Rape you.
Bite you till you bleed. That's the bill-of-fare. That makes sense to me.

                              BILLY
I've been practicing, dad.

                              LESTER
What?

                              BILLY
With a pillow.

                              LESTER
What are you practicing with a pillow, Billy?

                              BILLY
Ramming. The stroke. Smoke a jay. Pretend the pillow's your hard butt. I'm
really puttin' muscle in my pelvis with the pillow. Look. Feel.

                              Billy pulls off his tank-top. Pulls down the
                              waist of his sweat pants to the pelvis.

                              LESTER
Beautiful. Yes. I miss these.

                              BILLY
You can have them back. Anytime.

                              LESTER
Have you missed me?

                              BILLY
All the time. The team's great. Not like us. We only get to play any more when I
bring a new boy over. I get jealous when you do another boy.

                              LESTER
I crave the challenge of a stranger.

                              BILLY

Sometimes I wish you'd let me kiss you... all over.

                    LESTER
Billy, stop. Listen. I miss our regular sessions more than you know. I want to
tear off your pants, pin you, ravish with my fat dick... That's a given.

                    BILLY
Be tender with me, dad. I'm your son.

                    LESTER
There's something wrong with my blood. Dr. Fritz found this anomaly in my
sperm.

                    BILLY
Booby prize from Bangkok?

                    LESTER
Billy!? Nothing he's seen before. That's why I've been confining my activities to
the boys you bring home. I figure, hell, does it matter, I'm gonna kill them
anyway. Fuck 'em all night. What's the difference? A dead issue.

                    BILLY
All the more reason. I should do you for a change.

                    LESTER
You fuck me, you gotta fight me first. And you're not strong enough, yet, to
take me.

                    BILLY
Some day I will be.

                    LESTER
When that day comes, son, you can fuck me all night.

                    BILLY
Let me show you what you're missing.

                    LESTER
Show & Tell.

                    BILLY
Can I use your pillow?

                    LESTER
Here?

                    BILLY
Should I take off everything to show you, or tease you in my sweats.

                              LESTER
Tease me in your sweats!

                              BILLY
Watch me ram this pillow. Tell me if you're not impressed.

                              LESTER
Okay. Okay. I'll write a review for the Times. Show me already, you fuckin'
nut!

                                        By flashlight, BILLY rapes a pillow to a
                                        frenzy, till he cums, while a saxophone
                                        wails in the background.

                              BILLY
Well. What do you think?

                                        Billy throws the cum-stained pillow to his
                                        father. LESTER smells pillow deeply &
                                        faints.
You okay? Daddy?

                              LESTER
                              (comes to)
Everyhing's jake. What am I, but an old surrogate for all you poor souls out
there in the dark, who can't touch him as I can.

                              BILLY
                              (looks at the
                              flashlight beams,
                              the great dark)
What souls? Where dark?

                              LESTER
The eyes of time, Billy. History.

                              BILLY
History records.

                              LESTER
What we do in this place vanishes in the time it takes to say this line.

                              BILLY
We're not in a movie.

                              LESTER
Real time.

                              BILLY

The time that passes...

LESTER

And won't come back to haunt us...

BILLY

Only in our minds.

LESTER

And when the mind goes...

BILLY

There goes memory.

LESTER

Goodbye History.

BILLY

You and me, dad.

LESTER

Father and Son.

BILLY

No witnesses.

LESTER

I pray to god I live long enough for you to beat me, Billy.

BILLY

Let me come on your ass, dad. Be my pillow.

LESTER

When I'm done with Brewster Willson you can pump your cock against my ass
till you cream, okay?

BILLY

You won't be disappointed, pop.

LESTER

You'd better go back to practice. You'll be missed. Work on Willson for
Saturday. Tell him you got an extra set of dumbbells you'll give him. Worked
before.

BILLY

Yes. I will. (a pause) Can I kiss you?

                    LESTER
Men don't kiss, Billy.

                    BILLY
Can I rub myself against you then, just a little...

                    LESTER
As long as there's no romance intended.

                    BILLY
I'll try. I promise. I love you so.

                    LESTER
And I you, Billy. In my fashion.

                              THE FATHER stands in front of his son.
                              The Son embraces the FATHER. Rubs his
                              body against his father. Harder. Till he
                              cums.

                    BILLY
YOU'RE MY FATHER. I'M YOUR SON. LOVE ME. LOVE ME. LOVE ME.

THE FATHER IS A STATUE.

BLACKOUT.

SCENE 5: AN EARLY PAGE FROM THE BOOK OF BILLY

                              BILLY
Daddy, Daddy.

                              FATHER

                              (jumps up from
                              chair)
Billy! Come down. I'm home.

                              The sound of a boy's legs running
                              downstairs.

Oh , god! Gve me the strength for this.

                              BILLY bursts into the room, in shorts, oiled.
Hi, son.

                              BILLY
I'd hug you , Daddy... but... evergreen oil.

                              FATHER
I see. And smell. Did you do this for me?

                              BILLY
Yes. For you. Do I look... nice?

                              FATHER
Nice? (pause) Nice? (a pause, then distractedly) Dreamy.

                              BILLY
Huh?

                              FATHER
Where's Mom?

                              BILLY
At group.

                              FATHER
The traffic from the airport was hell.

                              BILLY
You look great. How was Thailand?

FATHER

Experience of a lifetime, Billy. Can't wait to go back. Someday, when you're big, I'll take you.

BILLY

I'm big, now. The coach said so.

FATHER

What?

BILLY

He said, "You got real meat on those bones, boy!"

FATHER

He did?! "Real meat"?!

BILLY

Told me I had sturdy loins for a lad of 13.

FATHER

Loins?

BILLY

What's "loins," dad?

FATHER

Your pee-pee and its environs.

BILLY

Oh. (pause) Is that good?

FATHER

Evidently the coach thinks so or he wouldn't have said it. Over-developed Polish boy-fucker's gonna get himself killed he touches my boy's body in any way.

BILLY

Don't get mad, daddy. I'm the new boy on the team. Sawicky wants to encourage me. I got the best body. He's a really nice guy... the coach... and wow, can he wrestle!

FATHER

WHAT?!

BILLY

Almost as tough as you, pop.

FATHER

What?!

BILLY

While you were away, we wrestled every day. Taught me a lot. Got hard like you, down there, like you. Only difference, he don't bite my legs and lick my ears like you do... and...

FATHER

Billy! Stop!

BILLY

Sure, Dad.

FATHER

I'll take care of Coach Sawicky. You take care to listen to what I tell you. Billy-- stand still. Stop flexing. Listen to me.

BILLY

You like when I flex.

FATHER

Yes, I do and you will and we'll wrestle and all the things we've done before we'll do again. I need for you to hear what I must tell you.

BILLY

Tell me, Daddy.

FATHER

I had an epiphany in Bangkok.

BILLY

Is that like falafel?

FATHER

No, Billy. An epiphany's like nothing in Heaven or Hell. Beyond time. Outside all experience as we know it.

BILLY

I don't understand.

FATHER

Come to me, Billy.

BILLY comes to his father.

BILLY

Yes, Daddy.

                                        FATHER
Billy. I love you.

                                        BILLY
Sure you do. You're my daddy.

                                        FATHER
No, Billy. I love you.

                                        BILLY
Thanks.

                                        FATHER
I love you more than "Thanks." More than mom.

                                        BILLY
More than mom?

                                        FATHER
I want you with me every moment, Billy... wake up in the morning with you in
my arms, not your mother. I want you to move in with me.

                                        BILLY
Huh?

                                        FATHER
Ever heard of LSD, Billy?

                                        BILLY
Move in with you?

                                        FATHER
This marriage is dead, you know that. Can't stand for her to touch me.

                                        BILLY
You're not gonna divorce mommy, are you?

                                        FATHER
Where would she go? She's on so many pills, she can't find the toilet. The night
I left, she pissed in the sink.

                                        BILLY
Mom's sick.

                                        FATHER
She's a junkie, Billy, an alcoholic nymphomaniac.

                                        BILLY
Sings the blues like nobody's business. Don't break up with mommy, Daddy.

FATHER

I won't leave your mother, Billy. I can promise you that. Alright?

BILLY

Promise.

FATHER

I did already.

BILLY

Okay. Thanks.

FATHER

You'll move your stuff to the master bedroom. Mom can take the spare on the second floor. We'll move the mats & weighs from the attic to the garage, save the cellar for little parties with your boyfriends... I mean, the guys on the team.

BILLY

Parties?

FATHER

Wrestling soirees, body-building competitions, spitting contests...

BILLY

Spitting?

FATHER

Can you keep secrets, Billy?

BILLY

Sure.

FATHER

If I told you a secret that could hurt your daddy bad if it were known, could you keep a secret like a rock in your guts, and never tell?

BILLY

For my daddy, you bet!

FATHER

I had a lot of sex over there, Billy, with young boys.

BILLY

As young as me?

FATHER

As young as 12.

BILLY

You said rubbing dorks with me like we do, would keep you off the boys.

FATHER

On my side of the family the men are very horny. My father kept boys in style in nice rooms all over Red Bank, New Jersey.

BILLY

How many?

FATHER

Who knows? Dad was a respected pediatrician. Had his pick of the litters, I'd say. A 40-year practice... you watch 'em grow up, fill out, sprout hair in all the appropriate places...

BILLY

Not grandpop. You. In Thailand. How many boys?

FATHER

Quite a few and many times until the night the epiphany took me.

BILLY

What's zat?

FATHER

Took acid with Russell Moffler, the second night of the tour. Had four boys the day we arrived. We fought. I fucked 'em. Two bucks. Bye-bye. The acid changed all that. For the first time I felt separated muscle on my body... everywhere... as never before, I was... alive! I went nuts, Billy.

BILLY

Nuts, pop?

                    BILLY offers a bag of peanuts to daddy.

FATHER

No thanks. (pause) Popcorn? (offers a bag to BILLY)

BILLY

I will. (takes a handful) Thanks. Go on.

FATHER

Hit the streets like the wrath of God. Went to the bath house, shot wad after wad on the hard bodies of Thai boys. No fuck. Too slow. I was... furious!

BILLY

You mean, angry.

FATHER

I mean, <u>furious</u>! A wild animal at bay. Could <u>not</u> stop grinding my teeth I was so... hungry!

BILLY

You shoulda packed a sandwich.

FATHER

Didn't have to. Was surrounded by fresh meat.

BILLY

You had sex in a restaurant?

FATHER

I had an epiphany.

BILLY

You mean, appetizer.

FATHER

I mean, epiphany, you silly little shit! I... ate three boys.

A long pause.

BILLY

Three boys?

FATHER

Yes, Billy. Yes. (short pause) And they were good, too.

BILLY

You shoulda ate before you came. That's too many boys.

FATHER

Billy!

BILLY

Yeah, pop?!

FATHER

I'm confessing to you!

BILLY

Yeah. Right.

FATHER

I crushed, stomped, and ate 3 boys.

                                    BILLY
You beat 'em, right?

                                    FATHER
Yes.

                                    BILLY
In a fair fight. Body to body.

                                    FATHER
Ah-huh.

                                    BILLY
You squeezed 'em, right...?

                                    FATHER
Of course.

                                    BILLY
Kicked 'em around a little.

                                    FATHER
That's right.

                                    BILLY
One thing. Did you kill 'em before you ate 'em? 'Cause, a <u>real</u> animal goes for
live meat.

                                    FATHER
Stop. Billy!

                                    BILLY
What feeds on death but maggots, pop. A strong man like you with such a tough
and desperate body wants his meat raw, still pumping blood, still wrestling.

                                    FATHER
Where did you hear that, Billy?

                                    BILLY
From grandpa.

                              A shocked silence.

                                    FATHER
Billy?

                                    BILLY
Yes, daddy?

FATHER

I really need to fuck you now, son. The time has come.

BILLY

I've been waiting so long for you to ask me, dad. Wanna wrestle?

FATHER

Sex is best for all concerned when one, at last, submits.

BILLY

Make me submit, poppa. Fuck me.

FATHER

We never went this far before, Billy. I'm nervous.

BILLY

I'm not. Take my ass, daddy. Slam me up against the headboard in the guest room.

FATHER

How could you get so sophisticated in two weeks?

BILLY

You shot all over me a hundred times, nearly killed me half a dozen more before I was twelve. I jerk off six, eight times a day... no good... I want you, dad. Only you. I will move in with you. Fuck Mom. And believe me, I plan to.

FATHER

Billy! What did you do with my father?

BILLY

Grandpa and me screwed around in the rec room at the Nursing Home before he died.

FATHER

Why do you spring this on me now, when I need for you to be the innocent I always thought you were?

BILLY

I can be innocent if you like, pop. I can be anything you want? Let me show you what I can do. Gimme a chance. You can't find a tighter fuck than me. Tighter than Thais. Grind my ass, dad. Plug my hole!

Daddy does.

FATHER

Oh my god! Billy! I could eat this butt for breakfast.

BILLY

On whole wheat toast?

FATHER

With grape jelly.

BILLY

Squeeze me, Daddy. Make my cock hard.

FATHER

Yes, Billy, yes.

BILLY

Crush me, daddy. Beat me, daddy. Fuck me, daddy. I'm yours. Billy. Son.
Lover. Geisha. One Night Stand.

FATHER

Forever.

BILLY

I'm too little. You're too strong. Too big, poppa. Please don't stick this in me,
you'll kill me.

FATHER

Sonny Boy. Billy Baby. So hot. So young. So white.

BILLY

So what? I'm alive. Fuck me.

FATHER

You betcha, bubble-butt, I will.

BILLY

Welcome to the Billy Battersall School of Innocence & Design. Kiss me. Bite
me. Fuck me. You're my father.

BLACKOUT

SCENE 6: THE HAIRLESS HEINY... PART II... LESTER BATTERSALL, RED BANK, N.J. AND HIS ESCORT, ROVER, PREPARE TO HAVE A PARTY IN BANGKOK.

                              LESTER
We got poppers, fish line, chains, handcuffs, tit clamps, a few good toys, Tonka trucks, a Slinky and egg slicer...

                              ROVER
Why egg slicer?

                              LESTER
For the testicle salad.

                              Long pause while Lester takes a belt of
                              Southern Comfort and passes out. The clock
                              ticks in the silences.

Then, to Rover, from the floor:

                              LESTER
Help me up.

                              ROVER
Don't ... die on me! You okay?

                              LESTER
I feel unstructured. A suit made in Singapore.

                              ROVER
Can you stand?

                              LESTER
Have I legs? Where are the bbboys?

                              ROVER
I'll get one for you tout suite, woof woof, sir.

                              LESTER
I'm terrified.

                              ROVER
Of what? This place was made for a creep like you. Put yourself in my hands. You want coffee, tea? A dozen doughnuts.

                              LESTER
I'm fucked.

ROVER

Who isn't?

LESTER

I'm in terror...

ROVER

Don't be scared. Rover's here. woof woof... [sic]

LESTER

... OF MY LIFE!

ROVER

You'll feel much better about your life once you kill a boy. Let me fetch you one.

LESTER

When the "process" is about to start, the revels begin... that's the hardest moment of all, Rover.

ROVER
(goes for the direct
approach)

Let me feel your arms, sir... yeah... that's it... you're more than fit for the task, sir... you're a tough man. You can crush an Asian boy with these you know you can... Strong. Hot. Brutal. Unstructured. I gotta boy for you. Take two seconds.

LESTER
(frantic to be heard)

Listen, Rover. Heel. In Red Bank my father was everybody's favorite baby doctor. For 62 years. They were born, grew old and died and still dad delivered, as many as ten a day after The War. Boom years for babies. Then there were the abortions. Did them at night in the garage. The old place, out by Lake Morpheus. Saw him rip a fetus by hand from the belly of a black girl. Never got pregnant again. Never wanted to. Ran off with Father Divine. Dr. Battersall was a very progressive pediatrician. He taught me of the Will, and the Spirit inside the Will. Wasn't five years old, had me lifting weights, jacking off in little jars...

ROVER
(his mouth open for
some time)

... Little jars...? [sic]

LESTER

In coffee, face cream, pick-me-up, what have you.

ROVER

AHH...look... I can ring for an attendant... there's good baklava from the snack bar... coffee.

LESTER

Shh, Rover, shh. After papa founded Boy Love Incorporated in '46, the house was full of other people's children, at all odd hours... They waited for him... so patient and sweet... trusting and young... stood in line, so quiet, one by one he took them all... he took the town.

ROVER
(stunned by the
revelation)

Your father is The Master Whang?

LESTER

Sure is, all 17 inches. You read the newsletter.

ROVER

Never miss an issue. Wanna stay up to date on what's "out there."

LESTER

At 17, he took me to the Jersey Turnpike and pointed. "Go. Fill in the holes." And I did. Twenty years or more of filling holes and when he wanted a grandson, I gave him Billy. Perfect in every way. No conscience whatsoever. That's my Billy. I love him. Everyone does. My dad and I made him the miracle he is. I call Billy, The Will Immortal. My dad... daddy... papa... CALLS him...

ROVER

What does Master Whang call Billy?

LESTER

Floor sample.

ROVER

You mean, prototype?

LESTER

What can be achieved through diet, exercise, herbal douches and violent sex. Started him out at a year and a half, one finger at a time, twice a day. By the time he was six, could take my open hand to the second joint, fist to the wrist. Amazing. Feathers, fruits and vegetables... household tools... a plastic Slinky... all this and more found their way up Billy's butt. Hung him in the closet upside down at bedtime... His eyes bled, yes they did and his ears... Still, soaking one's brain in blood every now and then renews the mind. Master Whang said so. Draws the pain from the testicles, the torn bunghole... the engorged sac... Every bone in his body was systematically broken and re-set... The trauma made him strong. Starvation, tight & wary. My Billy has borne his torments with grace, humility and courage... like a dead President. A murderous Young Lion, tested in all that hurts & mars... again & again. I challenge him to scream in agony or terror. He won't. Indestructible. Unfeeling. A beautiful beast. That's Billy.

ROVER

And where is The Master Whang... the good doctor... your fabulous father?

LESTER

Rest Home in Englewood. His mind is largely gone. His body remains remarkably intact. Unchanged. As though God himself approved and left my dad forever over-sexed... unsatisfied... with the body of a boy and the brain of an infant... All god took was the mind of him. Fucks like a bunny at the nursing home. Can't remember he came or why. Always wants to. Does. Seventeen inches of elderly cock, the head the size of a Bermuda onion... You get a piece of equipment that size spraying good-size room! Man alive, my dad drops his load in every corner. The bed pillows sodden with smegma. All his socks are stuck together under the bed. His quarters reek of sex, death and young men drowning in flop sweat an shit. My papa's great pole fucking boys... all day... all night if they didn't knock him out... fucking fucking. And for the life of him... Our Master Whang... the good doctor... my fabulous father... Doesn't know why. Why. Why.

(a pause. the clock
ticks)

Oh my God! Christ Almighty!

ROVER

What now? What's wrong?

LESTER

Nothing. Got myself back to where I belong. I'm ready for a boy now. Feel my cock.

ROVER

Oh, yes. What got you hard? Talking about Billy or your father?

LESTER

Both. I think of them, I get hot, can't help myself. Ya know, FAMILY. I need to break the back of a young boy... tonight... Now. Fetch, Rover.

ROVER

At your pleasure, sire. I'm your dog. I fetch a boy for you, woof woof.

LESTER

And if you bring a nice young smooth one, with a heiny as hairless as ou promised... you can share in the scraps... Whatta ya say, Rover, let's party.

BLACKOUT

SCENE 7: SATURDAY MATINEE AT THE BATTERSALL FAMILY HOME. BILLY AND HIS DAD THROW A PARTY FOR THE WRESTLING TEAM FROM RED BANK HIGH.)

> Dad enters kitchen, smoking a joint. Dad is dressed in sweatpants, bra, and a fright wig.

> DAD
> (yells into the
> basement)

Take a break, boys. Be right down. Put the weights back on the racks. Relax on the mats. Billy, pass out the Hi-Pro fruit bars, Hawaiian Punch and Xtasy tabs. Just spread out, guys. Think about how good your bodies feel... young, tough, pumped. Peter! Don't play with your porker, I'll take care of that.
(then to himself)
This is great! Better than ever! Billy! Come up here, I need you.

> BILLY
> (still in the
> basement)

Dad! Pete's pulling at himself again!

> DAD
> (yells down the
> cellar steps)

You jack-off before the rest of us, Pete, I gotta tell ya, automatic suspension.

> PETE
> (in the basement)

Billy's gotta hard-on, too, Mr. Battersall.

> BILLY

Fuck you, Pete, I'm always hard.

> PETE

And Dale's gotta boner, too.

> DAD

So what, we all do.

> Murmurs of assent from the basement.

> DAD

Calm down, guys. You got ten minutes before the games begin. Stay hard. Concentrate. Don't touch your pubes, Billy. Come up.

> Billy enters, in tight shorts with a boner.

                                   DAD
Frisky bunch, Billy.

                                   BILLY
All hot, like I promised, daddy.

                                   DAD
This is the largest load of lads you've ever brought me, Bill. I'm impressed.

                                   BILLY
Checked 'em out in the showers like you told me. The best bodies I could find.
For you, too.

                                   DAD
And they all have nice big testicles.

                                   BILLY
And fat peckers, papa.

                                   DAD
If the awards committee from Boy Love Incorporated could see us now...

                                   BILLY
We'd take the trustees' citation, hands down, dad.

                                   DAD
I'll bet you, Billy, no other member in the metropolitan area has screwed four
junior high school wrestlers in a single afternoon...

                                   BILLY
And his own son, don't forget me, pop.

                                   DAD
You're right. Five.

                        He holds up four fingers.

                                   BILLY
You're a hot man, daddy.

                                   DAD
Get the acid for me.

                                   BILLY
The freezer?

                                   DAD
Under the fudgecycles.

BILLY

Got 'em, pop.

DAD

Twelve tabs should do it. In the punch.

BILLY

Can I take two now, dad?

DAD

Wanna get the edge on the other guys, dontcha, ya little devil.

BILLY

Nobody beats Billy on acid.

DAD

Except daddy.

BILLY

My daddy's a man. No boy beats Billy.

DAD

'Cause my Billy's the best.... right?

BILLY

Right as the rain on a swan in shit, pop.

DAD
(hands Billy a joint)

Huh? Here, take a drag.

                    Mom enters.

MOM

Did somebody die? Why are the blinds drawn? Les?

                    Billy whips the tablecloth off and wraps it
                    around his waist to hide the boner.

MOM

Lester. Billy. Turn on some lights, for God's sake.

BILLY

Mom, you're not supposed to come home till six on Saturdays.

MOM

Dr. Fritz and half a dozen others got the flu. No group. Went by the Acme for
fish sticks. Got carried away. The car's full, Billy. Bring in the bags. Les, turn
on some lights.

                              DAD
The fuse is blown.

                              MOM
So pull up the blinds.

                              DAD
Fuck it, what's the use!

                                        Turns on lights.

                              BILLY
Dad! Don't!

                              MOM
I thought you said the fuse... (sees her husband for the first time) What are you done up for, Halloween?

                              DAD
The movie not the holiday. Ha ha. Just kidding. We're practicing.

                              MOM
For what? Mardi Gras?

                              BILLY
The spring concert.

                              DAD
I'll take care of this, Billy.

                              MOM
Lester, you look nuts.

                              DAD
Billy, get the bags.

MOM
He's not going out to the car in a tablecloth, wearing a wig.

                              BILLY
I'll do it fast, Mom.

                              MOM
Lester! Stop him. The neighbors.

                              DAD
I'll go, Estelle. We have to talk.

MOM

You'll go? You look crazier than Billy.

BILLY

We're ah ah... rehearsing!!!

MOM

What?

DAD

In a very short time, dear, Billy and I will appear quite mad to you...

MOM

You appear quite mad to me now. Why wait? What's going on here? Look, there's ice cream melting in the trunk. Will one of you please put on something normal and get the goddam bags out of the car?!?

DAD
(makes a decision;
not for Christ)

Billy, take off your shirt.

BILLY

But pop, my... you know... you don't want Mom to see my...

DAD

She has to see this sooner or later.

MOM

What are you talking about?

DAD

Show your mother how you've grown, son...

BILLY

Aw dad, I wish we didn't have to do this...

DAD

I want your mother to know what I have to contend with every Saturday afternoon. Show her.

BILLY

Oh boy, pop, is this ever embarrassing.

He drops the tablecloth to reveal the
enormous boner in his shorts.

MOM

Heavens to Betsy, what the hell is <u>that</u>?!

> Peter enters from the basement, his
> shorts similarly bloated.

PETER

Hey coach: when are we gonna wrestle? Hi, Mrs. Battersall.

MOM

Peter! Billy! Put those things" away.

DAD

Don't touch those dicks, boys. They're mine!

MOM

Lester!

DAD

What!?

MOM

Both those boys have erections!

DAD

And fat nuts! Don't forget those!

MOM

This is insane!

BILLY

This is a party, Mom.

PETER

For Dale. His birthday.

MOM

Kitty Olivetti's Dale?

BILLY

He's fourteen today.

PETER

Dale's got big balls, too, Mrs. Battersall.

PETER & BILLY

(AS ONE)

We seen 'em.

DAD

Me, too. Like a pawn shop. Take off your coat, Ruth. Stay awhile.

MOM

How many boys with hard-ons are in my house, Lester? And don't play games with me, I'm pissed. We play bridge with Kitty & and Ward Ollivetti, you crazy man!

DAD

What's crazy about young men letting off some steam in a manly way with other men?

MOM

You're a grown man and a father, you fool! These are boys! You can't get away with a thing like this in Red Bank, N.J. Their fathers work at the mill. They'll kill you!

DAD

Jesus Christ, Ruth, don't be so goddamned judgmental about something a woman can't possibly understand. Or comprehend.

BILLY

Can I give Pete a couple tabs of acid, dad?

DAD

Sure, son. Give Wee-Wee and Warren four apiece. Dale's already stoned on airplane glue.

MOM

Airplane glue??!!

DAD

Take it easy, Ruth.

MOM

I will not! You're giving acid to these kids!?

PETER

There's coke & grass in the laundry room if you want some, Mrs. Battersall.

BILLY

And Hawaiian Punch.

MOM

Don't make jokes, Billy.

DAD

Okay, both of you, into the basement. The bare-assed wrestling begins in...
(looks at his wrist to check the time)
I left my watch on the work bench. What time is it, Ruth?

                              MOM
Time to call the cops. Billy. Peter. Put on some clothes.

                              DAD
Go down and oil each other's bodies, boys. Save the thighs for papa.

                             BILLY
Daddy's got dibs on the thighs...

                             PETER
Yeah, you told me. I get twenty bucks, right?

                             BILLY
Right. Twenty. Trust me. And the time of your life.

                        They go down.

                              DAD
Sturdy body that Peter's got... Helluva set of buns on him, too. You noticed?

                              MOM
Notice? Lester! Look at me!

                              DAD
Wanna try the acid, Ruth This afternoon will be a whole lot more fun for you if
you'll just get into the spirit of the thing...

                              MOM
"Spirit of <u>what</u> thing??!!" Child molestation?!

                              DAD
                       (gently, as though
                       nursing a child)
No, Ruth[. Boy Love.

                              MOM
Do you want me to scream?

                              DAD
I want you to relax, hon. Pop a few tabs with me, have some punch and watch
me roll around on the mats with the kids. They're hot when they're high.

                              MOM
Lester, we go to Bible study with their parents.

DAD
(waxes nostalgic)
You know, hon, my dad delivered their fathers, and had sex with all of them in their teens. God, Estelle, my dad, Doc Battersall, founded Boy Love Incorporated.

MOM
Are you hallucinating? Your father was a saint.

DAD
So I'm told. I wouldn't know. He had a taste for little boys and cold cuts. Could eat a pound of boiled ham a day, no cholesterol. The kids kept him young. Fresh butt was good for him, he said, and who was I to argue? At 91, he still blew boys in the back of our old Buick, that's why the seats were always sticky.

MOM
You're a MANIAC!

DAD
Smoke a joint. You'll feel better.

MOM
Lester, I'm in recovery.

DAD
You used to be so much fun to hang with on speed.

MOM
Do you know what these years of sobriety cost me?

DAD
In terms of what?

MOM
Everything, you dissipated dick head!

DAD
Hey hey hey. Watch your language.

MOM
I let my Billy go. I had to.

DAD
I'm grateful for that, Ruth.

MOM
You never touched me after I had my tubes tied.

DAD
My father told me, "A barren woman drives a man to boys every time," and he was right. I ask you, was he?

MOM
How can you think like this?

DAD
You failed me as a wife. God knows, your addictions fritzed Billy. What was I to do? I raised him. Trained him. You saw that boy's package, Ruth. You can thank me for that.

MOM
Thank you? What have you been up to all these years, behind my back, with Billy?

DAD
Every night, from the age of nine, I pulled his peter and look how large it's grown.

MOM
You what?

DAD
I put that ass on him. That kid can take more of me than you could in your salad days, Ruth, and that's no lie. That butt of his is deep as a river, tight as Van Damme's, and nearer to God than Mother Teresa.

MOM
I think I'm gonna have a heart attack.

DAD
Sit down. Wanna beer?

MOM
No! I wanna wake up! This is a nightmare!

DAD
If this doesn't wake you up, then nothing will.

MOM
Let me catch my breath. (she gasps for breath) Before I call the madhouse or the National Guard, if it comes to that... answer me one question...

DAD
Sure, hon. But make it quick... the boys...

MOM
Where was I all these years you corrupted my son?

                              DAD
At group.

                         A deadly pause.

                              BILLY
                        (from the basement)
Dad, you better get down here. Dale just shot a healthy load all over my back.

                              DAD
Oh no. Wait. Hold it. Now look what you've done.

                              MOM
Done? I came home.

                              DAD
Then go away, or party with the rest of us as any decent woman would...

                              MOM
I should never have gone to California.

                              DAD
You bring up Altamont again, I'll puke, so help me!

                              MOM
Wont' be the first time.

                              DAD
We all puked back then, that was the scene. I gotta go.

                              MOM
You gotta stop, Lester. We're old junkies, for god sake!

                              DAD
Genetically I'm very sound.

                              MOM
And mad as Manson.

                              DAD
Suit yourself. You coming down?

                              MOM
Lester, I can't let you do this. For twenty years I've tried to put myself back
together and all this time you were falling apart. How do you think that makes
me feel?

                              DAD
If you had a shred of decency left, a scumbag.

                              MOM
I wanted to be an opera singer.

                              DAD
All I ever wanted was a weekend on a waterbed with Bruce Lee.

                              MOM
Will you stop or must I kill you!

                              DAD
What a choice. Look. There's poppers and wine in the fridge. Be sensible. This
is Battersall country, Ruth. My hometown. You're the one with the bad rep here.
You go raving through the streets, they'll lock you up. Figure you fell off the
wagon for good this time. I'll get the sympathy, you'll get the clink. Think about
it.

                              MOM
This is hell.

                              DAD
No, Ruth. This is Red Bank, New Jersey.

                              BILLY
                            (in cellar)
Daddy!

                              DAD
Yes, Billy.

                              BILLY
You gonna come down and play with us or what? There's a basement full of
horny boys down here.

                              DAD
Grease their cans for me will ya? The petroleum jelly is on the shelf over the
stereo.

                              BILLY
And bring down that album, will you, pop?

                              DAD
Which one?

                              BILLY
The Velvet Underground.

                              DAD
How about Sympathy for the Devil?

                         BILLY
Great!

                         DAD
You got it, Billy.
                         (turns to Ruth who
                         is comatose)
Now, there's a boy who appreciates good music.

                         MOM
BLACKOUT.

She faints and the lights go with her.

SCENE 8: THE MOMENT OF MORTAL TRUTH FOR DOCTOR PRATT. BILLY, THE HUSTLER, TAKES HIS FEE.

In the dark.

BILLY

You wore me out, Doc.

PRATT

I'm pretty beat myself, kid.

BILLY

In the dark, you sound like my father.

PRATT

I'm nobody's father, Billy.

BILLY

You don't <u>feel</u> like my father... you <u>feel</u> like a young, horny guy. Wanna try me again?

PRATT

Let's take a break. (pause) How many times did you cum?

BILLY

I lost count. You?

PRATT

Four. Surprised myself. God, you're hot.

BILLY

Wanna smoke a joint?

PRATT

Let me get the light.

Fumbles in the dark. Turns on the light. Pratt on his knees, his face directly over the lamp, the harsh light unflattering. Billy on his knees behind Pratt, Billy's chin rests on Pratt's shoulder, the young face, the old face, side by side, a two-headed man, each head a different age. Billy bites Pratt's earlobe. Pratt reaches behind him, his arm akimbo and begins to massage the back of Billy's neck.

                              BILLY
Yeah. You got strong hands, man.

                              PRATT
You want a massage?

                              BILLY
Let's smoke.

                              PRATT
Wasn't there some left from the last one?

                              BILLY
On the floor. There.

                              PRATT
Yeah. I got it.

                              BILLY
Want a soda?

                              PRATT
There's no soda... grapefruit juice & thirst quencher.

                              BILLY
Light up. You want something?

                              PRATT
Water.

                              BILLY
I like you, Doc, I really do. It's a shame...

                              PRATT
Huh?

                              BILLY
What?

                              PRATT
Why a shame?

                              BILLY
                            (a pause)
This night's gonna cost you, pops... plenty.

                              PRATT
No discounts?

                              BILLY
Hey, man, we been wrestlin' around, jerking off for... what time is it?

                              PRATT
Three o-clock.

                              BILLY
Five hours. I don't take checks.

                              PRATT
I don't carry that much cash...

                              BILLY
Then I'm gonna stick to you like shit on a golf shoe, until you do...

                              PRATT
Do what?

                              BILLY
Pay. Cash.

                              BILLY bites PRATT on the back of his
                              neck.

                              PRATT
Ow. Ha ha.

                              BILLY
Be right back. Don't smoke the whole roach, okay? Wait for me, daddy.

                              BILLY exits to kitchen. PRATT turns on the
                              radio, switches from one station to another,
                              till he finds one on which a song is
                              performed live onstage. PRATT sings along.
                              The song? THERE'S A KIND OF HUSH
                              ALL OVER THE WORLD

                              Before the song ends, BILLY re-enters. A
                              glass of water in one hand, a box in the
                              other. BILLY sings the second chorus of the
                              song with PRATT.

                              BILLY
                              (opens box)
What are these?

                              PRATT
Ampules. Put 'em back in the refrigerator.

BILLY

Speed?

PRATT

From the Institute.

BILLY

Oh. Don't get you high?

PRATT

Billy-boy, I'm a doctor. I do recreational drugs, I don't manufacture them. That's a vaccine I'm working on.

BILLY

For what?

PRATT

Put 'em back. Let's smoke.

They smoke.

BILLY

What's it for?

PRATT

Briefly, Billy, without getting too technical, the vaccines designed to block venereal infection, dissipate lethal anomalies in sperm.

BILLY

Does it work?

PRATT

More or less.

BILLY

What d'ya mean?

PRATT

I'm not sure. Good results in the lab. Whether it works in the blood, I can't say. I don't know. Put it back.

BILLY

Do you believe in God?

PRATT

You asked me that before.

BILLY

And you said, "Research."

                              PRATT
And you agreed.

                              BILLY
That's all you believe in?

                              PRATT
Yes. Research. <u>And</u> performance.

                              BILLY
Performance?

                              PRATT
Baby, there is not one human characteristic, quirk, configuration or compulsion
that is not a reflection torn form the dark, wrested from chaos by tacticians,
scientists, and the motion picture industry. I can't say God is dead, Billy, but <u>if</u>
he's not, in these times He's less a deity than an actor on hiatus.

                              BILLY
I don't understand.

                              PRATT
Neither do I.

                              BILLY
You gonna give me that massage?

                              PRATT
I'm so tired, Billy.

                              BILLY
I'll give you one then.

                              PRATT
That sounds great. My neck, and back.

                                        BILLY
Spread out.

                                        PRATT does. On his stomach.
                                        BILLY straddles him and begins to
                                        knead PRATT's back with his hands.

                                        BILLY
Where's the oil?

                                        PRATT reaches out for the massage oil by the mat,
                                        and hands it up to BILLY, who squirts a stream of
                                        oil onto PRATT's back.

                          BILLY
Doc?

                          PRATT
Ahhhh. Yes, Billy?

                          BILLY
Would you care if I decided to kill you?

                          PRATT
Hahaha. You are a strange boy.

                          BILLY
I'm serious.

                          PRATT
If I thought you were, I'd beat the shit out of you. I took you all night long.

                          BILLY
That was play, Doc, for sex. I'm talkin' murder, here, not fantasy trips.

                          PRATT
I scissored you into submission twice. YOu came all over my legs.

                          BILLY
Yeah, twice. I evened it up, remember?

                          PRATT
I let you win then, Billy, cause that's what you wanted. Give and take, kid. Win
some. Lose some. I let you take me.

                          BILLY
My dad lets me take him, too.

                          PRATT
You wrestle with your father?

                          BILLY
That's how I got into this... with my dad.

                          PRATT
Kinky.

                          BILLY
Every Saturday afternoon we'd wrestle in the garage, in the basement, on the
living room rug. He beat me more than I beat him...

                          PRATT
... AND that's why I remind you of him?

                              BILLY

Yeah. Only he liked to bite me.

                              PRATT

Yeah, so do you, like father like son.

                              BILLY

All over... pin me down... bite my biceps, back, breast, buns...

                              PRATT

The Four Big "B's." Your papa sounds wild.

                              BILLY

Bites all over my body, had to play hooky from gym. He hurt me. (pause) I feel
sorry for you, Doc.

                              PRATT

Why?

                              BILLY

Will you pay me?

                              PRATT

Do you really <u>want</u> me to, Billy?

                              BILLY

Don't matter, I'll take what I want when I'm done.

                              PRATT

With what? The massage? You leaving so soon?

                              BILLY

No. With the murder.

                              PRATT

Stop talkin' like an asshole, Billy, and do my lower back.

                              BILLY

I'm gonna eat you, Daddy.

                              BILLY opens his mouth wide and dives
                              open-mouthed into the back of PRATT's
                              neck. PRATT howls and rears up, BILLY
                              on his back. BILLY forces PRATT's arms to
                              his sides. PRATT goes down. IN a flurry of
                              savage attacks & violent parries, BILLY
                              chews PRATT's throat.

                              BLACKOUT

Lights up on Nicky at the piano. A romantic
American ballad.

BLACKOUT

SCENE 9: LESTER BATTERSALL GOES SHOPPING. BELOW HOUSTON. NYC

SALESGIRL

Good morning.

LESTER

Just looking.

SALESGIRL

Can I help you?

LESTER

Nice long johns.

SALESGIRL

Thank you. Handmade from scratch with edible fibers from Indonesia.

LESTER

Beautiful colors.

SALESGIRL

We dye here.

LESTER

Excuse me?

SALESGIRL

In the back... we do the "dying" here.

LESTER

Don't leave me out!

SALESGIRL

What?

LESTER

I'm not feeling all that well myself these days.

SALESGIRL
(gets the joke, and
giggles sweetly)

Oh my... yes... I see. Sometimes all this "dying" talk drags me down, too. And we're in retail!

                         LESTER
Yeah. Life's a bitch!

                         SALESGIRL
Nothing for me to do. Keep smiling. Keep dying.

                         LESTER
You're perky in a crisis.
(holds up a pair of long johns)
Got this one in a canary yellow!

                         LESTER
You're perky in a crisis.
(holds up a pair of long johns)
Whoa! No! Canary Yellow?

                         SALESGIRL
Oh, yes, bright colors. I guess we could come up with a good dead canary...
excuse me... a nice canary yellow dye for you, I'm sure.

                         LESTER
You do appliqué work on your long johns?

                         SALESGIRL
If you want, we will. Would be "extra." What did you have in mind?

                         LESTER
Could you sew on here... (shows her the crotch) say, a milky white dribble of
male sperm? Could you do that?

                         SALESGIRL
Ah... I suppose. (pause) Sure. Why not?

                         LESTER
You're very accommodating... thank you.

                         SALESGIRL
POOKIE aims to please.

                         LESTER
Who's POOKIE?

                         SALESGIRL
This... (takes in the store with her open hand) is POOKIE.

                         LESTER
Spooky, yes, you are. POOKIE I don't get.

SALESGIRL

My store is POOKIE. So am I. My card.

LESTER

Nice name. POOKIE. Easy to remember.

SALESGIRL

My father own business... from Taiwan. The designs & dyes are mine.

LESTER

You're very talented. Your papa must be proud. I'm Lester Battersall from Red Bank, N.J.

SALESGIRL

Oh. Nice. Welcome. Will you pay by cash or by card?

LESTER

One question?

SALESGIRL

Yes?

LESTER

In the back here... along the butt-hole... could you dye an earthy brown swath right there... ah... maybe dark brown? Would you do that?

POOKIE
(after a pause)

OOOOkay. We can do that... for sure.

LESTER

You know what corn, beats, cashews and pickled eggs look like, all mooshed together and... decayed?

POOKIE

Do I have to say? I can only guess. I give up. You got me.

LESTER

Could you sew a few vegetables in many subtle colors on the brown... that would make me very happy if you would do that... POOKIE. Would you do that? For me, POOKIE?!

POOKIE

I could and I would... this will take a lot of work... I mean... expensive... Look, Mr. Battersall, no offense... but... are you gonna wear these long johns... or suck 'em?

LESTER

Right now I haven't decided. I'm fifty years old , POOKIE, and theres a great deal more unwanted activity down there then I've yet gotten used to.

POOKIE

I see.

LESTER

I scratch my ass, a <u>lot</u> more, for one thing. Sneak a fart? I shit my pants. My dick leaks no matter how many times I shake it in the bowl. And I jerk off in my briefs twice, maybe three times more than usual for me. Now I ask you... if you were a man in my condition, wouldn't <u>you</u> be willing to pay an arm and a leg to get <u>yourself</u> a pair of long johns that would both camouflage your bodily indiscretions <u>and</u> announce publicly to the world...
Yes, I'm here
Yes, I'm queer
And nothing works!!!
Wouldn't you, POOKIE, BABY?? Wouldn't you?!

POOKIE

I gotta tell you, Mr. Battersall, you scare me.

LESTER

I don't mean to scare, I want to <u>share</u> with you this great adventure.

POOKIE

Adventure?

LESTER

You know "dying," on that we're both agreed.

POOKIE

Thank you. POOKIE aims...

LESTER

... to PLEASE. I know. Do you know <u>this</u>??

Whips out a knife in the shape of a carrot.

POOKIE

Looks like a carrot.

LESTER

Wrong, POOKIE! THIS IS DEATH!

LES quickly slashes POOKIE's throat. Her mouth flies open, her vocal chords severed, her hand grasps her neck, the blood oozes through her fingers. POOKIE is dead on her feet <u>before</u> she falls.

BLACKOUT

SCENE 10: THREE MINUTES AFTER THE SLASHING, LES RETURNS TO HIS CAR AND BILLY.

                              BILLY
Did you do the deed, Dad?

                              LES
I did, indeed.

                              BILLY
Was it good?

                              LES
Fast & efficient.

                              BILLY
How much?

                              LES
Couple hundred bucks.

                              BILLY
Wow! We can spend a whole weekend at the Wall Street Sauna.

                              LES
No Billy. This trip we hit St. Nicholas in Harlem.

                              BILLY
The Santa Claus Bath House?!?

                              LES
No Billy. <u>Black</u> butt. Wait'll they see you son... those niggers are gonna hop on your pale white buns like fleas in heat, Billy.

                              BILLY
Yeah. But... But... my hero... my... my...

                              LES
                              (helps him out)
Daddy.

                              BILLY
Yep! My DADDY saves me...

                              LES
Your hero.

                           BILLY
Your hero!!

                            LES
No Billy. Your hero, not my hero. I'm the hero, here...

                           BILLY
Right. My hero... my daddy smites the gentiles.

                            LES
No Billy. That's the Bible. This be Harlem. Your daddy smites the
motherfuckers.

                           BILLY
Yeah! And then?

                            LES
We come...

                           BILLY
On the dead bodies.

                            LES
Before...

                           BILLY
We burn their house down.

                            LES
You make me very hot, son. Let's blow this joint.

                           BILLY
Did you use the carrot this time or beat him to death with the hammer?

                            LES
She died by the sword.

                           BILLY
How many slashes?

                              LES holds up one finger... the middle finger.

                           BILLY
One! Wow! Wish I coulda seen that.

                            LES
She didn't make a sound. Died smiling.

                           BILLY

Huh?

                              LES
She died smiling.

                              BILLY
You cut a lady?

                              LES
Of course.

                              BILLY
I thought we did guys. (pause) We do girls, too? Ladies? Like... mom? Is that a
good thing to do, dad? I mean... won't Jesus get mad?

                              LES
Jesus has so much to be mad about, son, I'm sure a woman or two every once in
a while won't get his old nose out of joint.

                              BILLY
Whew! Now I understand.

                              LES
Simple rule of thumb to remember in these cases, Billy: We kill men for kicks.
We only kill women... for money.

                              BILLY
Gee, thanks for the clarification, pop.

                              LES
Any time, son. I'm here to serve. Kiss me.

                              BILLY
When I taste your lips, God roars.

                              LES
You poetic little trollop... come here.

            FATHER & SON COME TOGETHER IN A FURIOUS
            EMBRACE.

            BLACKOUT

SCENE 11: WOK STORMS INTO HIS DRESSING ROOM, BILLY AFTER HIM.

WOK

Stay away from me. Leave me alone.

BILLY

Let me talk to you.

WOK

There's nothing to say. I want <u>off</u> this picture, NOW!

BILLY

Please, Wok, don't be mad. Give me another chance.

WOK

I'm Bruce, you crazy protestant bastard... another chance? To what? Kill me?

BILLY

Love you. Begin at the top, before I brought you home and ate you with my dad.

WOK

No more, enough is too much! That fat bitch will pay!

BILLY

What fat bitch?

WOK

My agent.

BILLY

Oh. Hey, you got the tightest little body I ever hugged between my legs... Your Wok in every way but one!

OK

What's that?

BILLY

You're a live Phillipino, not a dead Thai.

WOK

Let's talk plain green monkey here, Billy. All that shit went down on the set, that was no joke?

BILLY

The whole truth and nothing but the truth, so help me Mishima.

                                  WOK
What do you know of Yukio Mishima?

                                  BILLY
I read about him in a brochure from Buena Vista U.

                                  WOK
You, too?

                                  BILLY
And the Hart Crane Memorial Christmas Pantomime. Wanna go?

                                  WOK
No! I do not! I want you to get out of my dressing room. (calls out, frantically)
SECURITY!

                                  BILLY
Come with me to Disney. Pleasure Island. Be my guest. I won't let Dad kill you.

                                  WOK
That actor's your father?

                                  BILLY
And vice-versa.

                                  WOK
This is a great deal more than a docu-drama, then?

                                  BILLY
Yep. Hard Copy. Inside Edition. The Real Story, all rolled into one.

                                  WOK
                        (pause, while this sinks in)
SECURITY!

                                  BILLY
There's no security on this picture, Wok.

                                  WOK
BRUCE!

                                  BILLY
All I want to do is fuck you nice and slow... hard... deep.

                                  WOK
                           (holds up ring
                           finger)
Look, for Christ's sake, I'm married!

_____

BILLY

So what?

WOK

I haven't swung your way in years.

BILLY

Bet you'd learn to swing again with the right kinda guy.

WOK

You're very sexy, Billy... you know that...

BILLY

So come with me to Disney. Gonna shut down the set for a week, till the new producer shows up from back East. You deserve a vacation.

WOK

I deserve a medal. You hurt me out there. Bit me. I'm a mess. You didn't squeeze me that hard in rehearsal.

BILLY

My dad brings out the worst in me. I'm sorry.

WOK

Sorry? I weigh 105 pounds. Look at you. You're a husky boy... I'm no wrestler.

BILLY

Wok could wrestle. I bet I could teach you. Then everything would be perfect.

WOK

Perfect?

BILLY

We could start from scratch, the two of us, and try again. I wove you, Wok.

WOK

Stop that! Look at me?! I'm Bruce Alamada, international film star, married, with children, and responsibilities. If what you tell me is true, not just L.A. horseshit, you're a homicidal maniac and so's your father. I'm reporting this production to the Screen Actors Guild, and will file a complaint with the first cop I can find. Now get out of here.

BILLY

Can you be honest with me?

WOK

How much more honest do you want me to be? I'm not going to Pleasure Island with you. You won't fuck me, in Disney... or anywhere else. Period.

BILLY

Look, Bruce. I'll make you a deal.

WOK

No deals. No dice. No Disney.

BILLY

I won't do the lines from the script, okay?

WOK

That's a relief.

BILLY

Just gonna stand here and show you my body.

WOK

I'd rather you didn't do that.

BILLY

Why?

WOK

Don't waste time tempting me.

BILLY

I won't move on you, promise. Touch me, feel me all over, climb me like a tree.
I defy you to caress my body and not want my body. I dare you.

WOK

Who could resist a challenge like that from a boy like you?

BILLY

You tell me.

WOK

I can't wrestle.

BILLY

I'll teach you.

WOK

You want people to want your body, don't you?

BILLY

Sure. What else is there?

WOK

Your skin is tight, like unripe mango.

                              BILLY
Move your body hard against mine, Wok. Rub me with your cock, Bruce.

                              WOK
This must stop!

                              BILLY
Then stop.

                              WOK
I can't.

                              BILLY
Why?

                              WOK
That first day, in make-up, I knew you'd be a problem.

                              BILLY
Up until the Death of Wok, we did all our scenes in one take.

                              WOK
I know.

                              BILLY
One take. Know why?

                              WOK
No. Tell me.

                              BILLY
Cause we fit together so nice, Bruce, your body and mine.

                              WOK
In the Phillipines they call me One Take Alamada.

                              BILLY
That doesn't explain how easy it was for me to do those scenes in the Rice
Bowl... with you... was a snap.

                              WOK
Surprised me, too, how... professional... you were.

                              BILLY
Hey, I'ma pro all the way. Only thing I'm amateur at, is acting. When I put my
body on the line in the public eye and don't gotta fake what's already here...
(grabs his own dick.)

WOK

... In abundance... (rubs Billy's cock with his thigh)

BILLY

Right. I'm top of the line.

WOK

Yes. Top of the line.

BILLY

The better toaster.

WOK

A more expensive cut of meat.

BILLY

Our scenes went good, cause we were good... Two hot, sexy guys gone ga-ga on each other...

WOK

We did look beautiful in the rushes...

BILLY

So did Moses.

WOK

What??

BILLY

Nothing. Forget it. Let me fuck you, please. I promise I won't phone the papers.

WOK

This is crazy! Stop talking crazy!

BILLY

Everything was fine until my father fucked us up. I tried to stop him.

WOK

He's too scary, Billy. Too strong.

BILLY

Yeah, pop spoils everything. Always. When I was little, he read a magazine article how broken bones, once healed, are stronger than they were before the break. So guess what my daddy does?

WOK

I don't want to hear.

                              BILLY

Broke every bone in my body, 'cept my neck and spine, by the time I was
thirteen.

                              WOK

Billy, no.

                              BILLY

One by one. Took me in the basement and squeezed me. That was <u>before</u> he got
into actually <u>eating</u> young boys.

                              WOK

Oh baby, baby.

                              BILLY

Sure, Bruce.

                              WOK

Do you know what your father is?

                              BILLY

I guess you would call him a homicidal maniac...

                              WOK

Yes, you <u>could</u> call him that...

                              BILLY

I sure picked up a lotta bad habits from him, didn't I?

                              WOK

Yes, you did.

                              BILLY

He wants to tell his side of the story to the world. Can you blame him?

                              WOK

Yes, Billy. I <u>can</u> blame him, and so should you! What you do with your father is
wrong, unnatural, repulsive. That you would make a movie of it... recreate your
crimes and play yourselves... that's the sickest part of all... that's beyond
madness, Billy. We're talking about <u>fundamental</u> evil.

                              BILLY

Disney bought the project. Dad made a very good deal... I got the part i went up
for.

                              WOK

Playing yourself?

                                BILLY
Right. Was tough, too, down to five guys at the end...

                                WOK
You had to audition to play yourself?

                                BILLY
Dad insisted.

                                WOK
I'm not surprised you got the part.

                                BILLY
Course, in the end, daddy had to kill four of them. The fifth got away. I got the
part and a two-year contract. This is my big chance.

                                WOK
To kill again?

                                BILLY
That's where you come in.

                                WOK
No, Billy.

                                BILLY
I want a second chance with Wok. I never got such a thrill before from any
other body but my poppa's... Wok was sexier for me than anyone should have
the right to be. If he were alive I'd tell him so, be good to him... a good lover, a
best friend. Wok could trust me & love me, always. If Wok wasn't dead, I know
I'd be in bed with him right now, and I'd let him fuck me if he wanted to...
sometimes, you know, just for a change of scenery... God! I'd be such a good
buddy... really. I would.

                                WOK
How can I help you, Billy?

                                BILLY
Come away with me to Disney for Christmas. Let me make the kind of love to
you that only comes in old books by dead people. I want to be your... hero.

                                WOK
Be my hero?

                                BILLY
Rescue you from dragons, dwarfs, assassins, my father...

                                WOK
You'd do that for me?

BILLY

If you be my Wok, and give me one more chance, I'll make you so happy, Wok, you'll see... I'll show you the kind of love a serial killer is capable of... what d'ya say?

BLACKOUT

SCENE 12: THE HAIRLESS HINEY, PART IV: LESTER GAMBOLS IN THE GARDEN OF SEXUAL DELIGHTS

                              CHEWY
POOKIE AIMS TO PLEASE!

                              Pookie descends on Lester Battersall

                              ALL
WHO'S POOKIE?

                              CHEWY
My place is Pookie.

                              LESTER
Spooky, yes, you are. Pookie I don't get! You bit me, you cunt!

                              CHEWY
You have the brass balls to drag your flabby white ass to Bangkok, use that
same line on me and expect to live???

                              LESTER
She's delusional, Pookie, you require psychological evaluation.

                              CHEWY
YOU SLASHED MY THROAT IN SOHO!

                              LEGS
Oh, no. Soho?

                              LESTER
I don't know what you're talking about.

                              CHEWY
Are you not Lester Battersall from Red Bank, New Jersey?

                              LESTER
I are.

                              CHEWY
Bad English. You mean to say, "I is."

                              LESTER
Is, am, was, are... So what?

                              CHEWY
And you don't recall the summer morning three years ago you came into
POOKIE's for long johns?

                                LESTER
I loathe long johns.

                                CHEWY
Who cares? Look what you did to me!!!

                                LESTER
Nice job. I know people would pay dearly for an extra set of lips.

                                CHEWY
YOU FUCK! I've had 14 operations to repair my face besides. My ears are
plastic. Nose courtesy of Goodyear. Tongue of St. Bernard. The flesh on my
skull & face is sheer cotton gauze dipped in rabbit-skin glue. Some nights, after
a strenuous workout with Wegs...

                                LEGS
That's LEGS, Chewy.

                                CHEWY
Sorry. Call me POOKIE.

                                LEGS
I like you better Chewy.

                                CHEWY
Get off my back, you frivolous monkey!

                                        Legs slinks away, glares at Chewy
                                        from a distance.
What was I saying?

                                ROVER
Something about workouts with Wegs...

                                LEGS
LEGS!

                                CHEWY
I can't afford to work up a good sweat... my face falls off! Peels like a poster in
a downpour on St. Marks Place!

                                LESTER
I'd like to see that.

                                        ALAPETIA roars back into the
                                        action.

ALAPETIA

The cops have two floors to go and you're bitchin' about your face!? Fuck you where you breathe, Chewy...

LEGS

I've tried that. No big deal.

CHEWY

I don't care about cops. Bought 'em off before... I'll buy them again.

ALAPETIA

That's you. What about us?

CHEWY

The Meat Locker is a concession, Alapetia. They may close the Hairless Hiney, the Locker lasts forever.

MANDY
(enters from Meat
Locker)

Madame Chewy, someone turned off the generator. The dead faggots are defrosting.

MINDY enters right behind MANDY.

MINDY

And the old Lesbian smells like Eva LaGalliene.

MANDY
(to MINDY)

You gonna tell me that sick old story about Hildegarde's white gloves, I quit. Madame Chewy, we can't hide customers in the Locker.

MINDY

The customers are in the Locker, Mandy.

MANDY

Where? I didn't see customers.

MINDY

Mandy, do you know the difference between dead faggots and live people?

MANDY

Sure. I'm from the West Village. I been to piano bars.

CHEWY

Will you two butchers please shut up!? Legs! Get the customers in here. I want everyone's attention. This degenerate American daddy...

LESTER

Call me Lester.

CHEWY

Call me POOKIE.

ALAPETIA

Call me Tuesday. This place is nutz. (starts to leave)

CHEWY

Dont' walk out on me, Alapetia. I want witnesses.

ALAPETIA

YOU wanna get busted, Chewy, be my guest. I'm gonna smoke a joint in the maze, try to get what's left of my head together.

CHEWY

You will be missing a major dismemberment here.

ALAPETIA

I see you cut up white folks before, Chewy. Don't impress me.

CHEWY

What if I gave you scrotum sautéed in duck sauce?

ALAPETIA

Thanks for the offer. I'll stick with catfish and grits.

LESTER

Scrotum in duck sauce, you say? Hm. I bet that's good.

CHEWY

I'm gonna rip you a new asshole, Mr. Battersall.

LESTER

Thanks. I could use a spare.

CHEWY

What is wrong with this guy?

ROVER

I told you, Madame, acid overdose.

CHEWY

That oughta make the tortures I have planned for him more excruciating

LESTER

For you, maybe.

                        CHEWY
You force me to kill you quickly, when my first impulse is to take my time.

                        LEGS
Let me soften him up for you, Lover.

                        CHEWY
Yes, Wegs. YEs. Look at my hands, all a-flutter. Nerves. Rage. Couldn't crush
his balls if I wanted to... and I do so want to. Seconal. Get me seconal.

                        ROVER
You came to the right place. I've got narcotics to die for. Prozac, librium,
elephant tranquilizers.

                        CHEWY
I'll take a baker's dozen of every drug you've got.

                        ROVER
Now you're talkin'. Step into my office.

                        ROVER spreads a sheet in the air. ROVER
                        & CHEWY step under it. They disappear to
                        do their business.

                        LEGS
I heard about you.

                        LESTER
No kidding.

                        LEGS
I've been in Boy Love Inc. since I was twelve.

                        LESTER
How old are you now?

                        LEGS
You gotta count the rings on my cock to find out.

                        LESTER
Is that a complimentary offer or will you make me fight for it?

                        LEGS
Fight.

                        LESTER
I like to fight.

                              LEGS
I hear you love to wrestle.

                              LESTER
I've had a goodly share of young men die in my arms.

                              LEGS
Who hasn't?

                              LESTER
Who won't?

                              LEGS
Don't ask. My job is to soften you for Chewy, and I will.

                              LESTER
I saw you earlier this evening... in the stairwell...

                              LEGS
I adore stairwells...

                              LESTER
... Toilets, glory holes, dark rooms in smelly places...

                              LEGS
What can I tell you, I'm a romantic.

                              LESTER
You were blowing a guy in a yarmulke.

                              LEGS
Rene. Piano player. Works part-time upstairs, in the The Cocksuckers Lounge.
When he's in town I blow him.

                              LESTER
The minute I saw you I wanted to kill you.

                              LEGS
Funny, I had the same feeling myself.

                              LESTER
All things come to him who waits.

                              LEGS
I'm into Boy Love big time.

                              LESTER

Love 'em and leech 'em, eh?

                              LEGS
I'll suck you dry.

                              LESTER
I'll fuck you to death.

                    RENE bursts in, followed by OTTO. RENE looks
                    like Sol Hurok on a budget. OTTO looks like a
                    Swiss tourist in the Bahamas.

                              RENE
You gotta tuned piano down here, I'll lick your ass.

                              OTTO
I told you already, Rene, I know this piano. Not only is it out of tune, the ass in
here is dead, and all the live butt may as well be.

                              LEGS
Rene!

                              LESTER
You're the Jew Legs blew in the stairwell.

                              RENE
Hum a few bars. I play by ear.

                              LESTER
Wanna blow me?

                              RENE
No thanks. White meat tastes like airplane glue.

                              OTTO
Rene's into color, hobby kits and tuned pianos.

                              RENE
Something is way wrong in show business when a creepy little jew with too
many fingers...

                              OTTO
... Not unlike yourself...

                              RENE
... has to work in a hole like the Hairless Hiney.

                              OTTO
Wait a minute. This was your idea.

RENE

Oh no no, Otto, a tour of Southeast Asia with Petula Clark... was your idea...

OTTO

Petula Clark's dresser... you never listen or let me finish. You got dusky dick on the brain, Rene. All I said was, "Wanna go to Bangkok?" You came in your pants at the prospect.

RENE

Not for Petula Clark's dresser...

PETULA CLARK's dresser enters, in spotless white, done up like your worst nightmare of A Virgin Run Amok.

PETULA

Where are my lead sheets? Never will I work outside the United Kingdom again.

OTTO

I don't mean to be a silly German shit, Pet, as I recall... you can't work in England.

PETULA

Politics. Fuck Sir Lew grade. I sang for the queen.

RENE

Elizabeth?

PETULA

Lord Snowden. Besides, everyone knew Sir Lew slept with Tommy Steele, was common knowledge. Even I knew...

OTTO

And God knows, you're common enough.

PETULA

Was all over RADA. Why should I be shipped off to Bangkok when everybody in the business back home knew the score? Vera Lynn Knew it, for Christ's sake. Is that the piano?

OTTO

Good guess.

RENE

Don't crack wise, Otto, she pays the bills.

PETULA

Clear the rehearsal hall.

OTTO

Is she kidding?

PETULA

Must we bargain with mongrels? Placate pimps? I must rehearse... NOW!

RENE

No problem, Pet.

<blockquote>MADAME CHEWY & ROVER throw off the
sheet, under which Chewy has besotted herself with
narcotics.</blockquote>

CHEWY

Yes, by all means, rehearse, and while you do, Lester and I will play. Wanna party, Mr. Battersall?

<blockquote>CHEWY stabs LESTER in the shoulder with a
carrot.</blockquote>

ROVER

Don't. He's a customer.

CHEWY

He's a killer!

PETULA

I don't care if he's the King of the Khyber Rifles. Play, orchestra, play.

<blockquote>ASHLEY interrupts from the audience.</blockquote>

ASHLEY

Don't you touch those ivories. The Troutwiens engaged that piano and nobody plays it but me... Besides, we have another hour on our rental agreement. Look. (whips out the rental agreement)

OTTO

Who are you?

ASHLEY

Ashley Wilkes from Waken, Georgia.

RENE

Let's no fight. We open tonight. We need the piano...

PETULA

110

I need the piano. I'm the headliner here.

CHEWY
The Meat Locker has nothing whatever to do with the Hairless Hiney. This is our sub-basement, not those wretched Japs who own this dump. Sing! Music and murder are my meat.

ROVER
I'm responsible for this guy, Madame Chewy. He's white, you can't kill him. I have an obligation to the Yellow Peril Escort Service...

ASHLEY
Brandon! Brenda! The piano is under attack. Come quickly. We must defend the keys from barbarians, Berserkers, Huns, renegade jews and one overbearing English cunt!

                              BRANDON & BRENDA burst out of the
                              light booth.

BRANDON
How dare they! I'm with Disney, an executive producer.

BRENDA
I wrote The Cat's Meow, a comedy for funerals and other inevitable events. Played for a year in Needles, California.

OTTO
Needles?! That's in the Mojave Desert!

                              While this dispute continues, LEGS &
                              CHEWY torture LESTER.

BRANDON
I produced CLEAN & JERK, a musical for Jocks. Smash hit at Gold's Gym in Torrance.

BRENDA
We sponsored a benefit for Little Black Sambo...

BRANDON
I have power lunches three times a week with Getha Bomboy, Sidney Firpo and Willy Fitz!

OTTO & RENE
WHO?

BRENDA

My father spent 25 years carving the entire "Rubiyat of Omar Khayam" on the head of a pin.

                          BRANDON
Interestingly enough, not one single word was legible. We're famous.

                          BRENDA
Rich.

                          ASHLEY
Cheap.

                    BRENDA & BRANDON
Here, here.

                          BRENDA
All I want is a dead Lesbian in a reasonable condition...

                          BRANDON
And a tuned piano.

                          CHEWY
                    (takes a break from
                    torturing Lee)
What the fuck do I care about Disney, dead Lesbians or tuned pianos?

                          RENE
Search me. Right now I could use a bagel with a shmear.

                          BRANDON
Disney's our meal ticket.

                          BRENDA
Dead Lesbians our obsession. [sic]

                          CHEWY
I was a good girl before this pestilential maggot cut me up! That I survived was a miracle. Now I have him, he's mine. He will suffer, endlessly, without surcease. Must I murder all of you? Sing or shut up. Let me do my worst.

                          RENE
We have a contract to perform in the snack bar.

                          CHEWY
This is not the snack bar, this is the Meat Locker.

                         OTTO
There are cops in the snack bar. We came directly from Chop-Socky Airport.
We are tired, jet-lagged.

                         PETULA
Might I suggest a compromise?

                         CHEWY
This is not a talk show!

                         EVERYBODY
That's what you think!

                    MINDY & MANDY re-enter.

                         MANDY
                    (as balloons are
                    popped backstage)
My God, the faggots are exploding! Methane!

                         MINDY
Over 80 degrees in the freezer. The Lesbian melted!

                         MANDY
This is a public health issue!

                         OTTO
Correction: this PLAY is a public health issue.!

                         MINDY
We're trapped.

                         MANDY
The only way out is "up."

                         OTTO
Up? We can't go up. The cops are up!

                    ALAPETIA re-enters.

                         ALAPETIA
The Maze is infested with fuzz. The only way out is "Down."

                         MANDY
We can't go down. We're as low as we can get!

                         ALAPETIA
There's the sewer!

MINDY

Alapetia's right. If the police have gotten as far as The Maze, that's one flight up. We're fucked.

OTTO

Hold it! I don't know about the rest of you, but...
Whenever I feel afraid
I hold my head erect

RENE

And whistle a happy tune...

PETULA

So no one will suspect I'm afraid... Hit it boys!

> THEY DO. MUSICAL NUMBER. Brandon & Brenda applaud wildly at the end of Petula's number.
>
> EVERYONE SCREAMS BLACKOUT!
>
> ANNOUNCEMENT IN
> THE DARK
> One Hour and Twenty Musical Numbers Later
>
> Lights up. AHSLEY, RENE, OTTO, BRENDA, BRANDON, and PETULA, high as kites, smoking joints, perform a medley of show tunes and unexpected ditties. Everyone else is either asleep or unconscious.
>
> At the end of the medley, BRANDON, BRENDA, OTTO, RENE, PETULA, and ASHLEY pass out.

A CACOPHONY OF MALE VOICES AT THE DOOR
MAYDAY! MAYDAY!
BANZAI
OIY VEY
EMERGENCY
RED ALERT
SOS
MEDICS
NURSE
MOMMY

ALAPETIA

Wake up, Chewy. Theres a mob outside.

                              CHEWY
There;s a mob inside, Beulah.

                              ALAPETIA
Don't insult your audience.

                              CHEWY
Don't crowd my Klling Ground!

                              VOICES
MOMMY!!!

                              ALAPETIA
Are you cops or cocksuckers?

                              ONE VOICE
Who's asking?

                              ALAPETIA
Don't shit me, Officer! I'm a Lenox Avenue Lilly, Alapetia Cashew to you. I rub
butt with Louie Farrakhan. I <u>know</u> cops! I <u>know</u> cocksuckers! I know who
<u>killed</u> Nicole! Don't try to slip no bad shit by me. Show me your badges. Throw
me a curve if you can. Grind my booty.
Is you is, or is you ain't COCKSUCKERS?! If you is, you in. If you ain't, you
out!

                              VOICES
ALRIGHT, ALREADY. WE ARE COCKSUCKERS!

                              ONE VOICE
Is this the place for Roy Cohn's Bar Mitzvah?

                              CHEWY
Open up. They're cocksuckers for sure. Let 'em in.

                              ALAPETIA
                              (presses an
                              imaginary button)
Come in, boys. Join the shit-heap. Canapés in the crapper. The maggots are on
the house.

                                        A CROWD of dressed and undressed
                                        folks of many colors enters. On a
                                        makeshift stretcher of sturdy arms,
                                        FARTS LEVECQUE, covered to the
                                        neck in a white sheet, is carried in,
                                        groaning and writhing.

ALAPETIA

Farts! Whatsa matter, baby, you sick?

FARTS

Save me, Jesus! Wipe my brow! I'm full of farts, Lord. Save me now. Don't be a bitch, Jesus! I went to Bible School. I sang in the Choir. Don't let me explode, Jehovah. My butt's obstructed, Bubba. I'm regusted. Whoa, Baby, whoa! Ahh!

ALAPETIA

Chewy! Do something!

CHEWY

Ah, whattsa matter, kid, you got somethin' stuck in your ass?

ALAPETIA

We know that! You're no help at all!

CHEWY

Can you do better?

ALAPETIA

Don't be coy, Farts. You've had everything but the kitchen sink shoved up your hole... Twice! I seen this shit from Farts before, Chewy. He wanna cadge free sympathy, the fuck! Reach up that big old crack o' yours and pull out what you stuck up in there.

CHEWY

Don't be coarse, Alapetia.

FARTS

I can't. I've tried.

ALAPETIA

What you got up that fat black butt of yours, girl?

FARTS

Frankly, I'm embarrassed to tell you. This much I'll say. He's got paws. Look.

> FARTS turns, drops the sheet or cloth of choice to display the entire arm and paw of a monkey, hanging out from between his buns.

EVERYBODY

Holy Christ! He's got a Monkey Up His Ass!

RENE

Better he should have a monkey on his back.

ALAPETIA
(aside to audience)

I'm almost afraid to ask.

(then to FARTS)

How did this happen?

FARTS

Why was I born?

ALAPETIA

That's the answer to another questions... from another show.

FARTS

Oh. Sorry.

ALAPETIA

Where does the monkey come from?

FARTS

Minnesota.

ALAPETIA

Who told you he came from Minnesota.

FARTS

The monkey.

ALAPETIA

Where?

FARTS

Where what?

ALAPETIA

Where did the monkey tell you he came from Minnesota?

FARTS

In the maze. Was love at first sight.

ALAPETIA

For you or the monkey?

FARTS

The monkey, you presumptuous black cunt!

ALAPETIA

Don't call me presumptuous, Farts!

FARTS

This monkey crawled up my butt before I knew what hit me! I was blowing a
cop. Saw this monkey watching me. Licked his lips and sniggered. Winked and
drooled. The cop came. I bit his dick. Blinked once and the monkey was gone.
Barely had time to swallow... WHAM! Never has fundament been plowed with
such fury and force! This monkey fucked me silly. Now loosen up and listen
hard, girls, 'cause this is straight poop I'm giving you... If you do not tear this
monkey from my ass... I'LL EXPLODE!

MANDY

Let's not play games here, Madame Chewy! As a biologist and sometime animal
lover, believe me... there is enough methane gas from decomposing faggots in
here...

MINDY
(butts in)
And the old dead Lesbian is virtually Dyke Soup...

MANDY
(butts in back)
Without the Marx Brothers...

MINDY
(double-butts him
one better)
If Farts explodes...

MANDY
(nutz by now)
This Meat Locker and all of US in it will blow sky-high.

CHEWY

We can't have that!

ALAPETIA

What the fuck, I left Harlem for this?! Gimme a straight razor... I know how to
handle stubborn monkeys.

MANDY

No cutting. Farts, could you tell us, Is the monkey alive?

FARTS

You know my condition, Mandy. I gotta fart. Kinda like my signature tune, and
I'm holding a big one all ready to go.

MINDY

Whatever you do, Farts, don't fart.

MANDY

Listen to Mindy. Is the monkey still alive?

                              FARTS
Oh... Oh... Oh... Oh my God!

                              MINDY
IS HE ALIVE?

                              FARTS
He got one long furry tongue... oh baby, you sure know how to work that thang!

                              MANDY
Is he licking you now?

                              FARTS
He's kissing my sphincter.

                              RENE
Is this Old Testament or am I a silly Jewish pippik?

                              OTTO
This is and you are. Excuse me while I vomit.

                              OTTO does, discreetly, into a white cotton
                              hanky. So does Ashley. Actually, several
                              people vomit.

                              MANDY
Listen to me, Farts. We must get that monkey out of your ass one way or
another, but you must not fart.

                              MINDY
You WILL not fart.

                              MANDY
We're gonna try to... ah... coax that monkey out of you...

                              MINDY
Yes! Ah... with crackers...

                              MANDY
And Beer Nuts!

                              ASHLEY
                              (shyly produces a
                              banana)
I gotta banana... Gotta bit of feces on the skin...

                                        (wipes the shit off
                                        the banana with a
                                        clean cotton hanky)
You're welcome to it. Here.

                    ALAPETIA
This is madness.

                    CHEWY
This is Bangkok.

                    MANDY
Bend over.

                    FARTS
Be kind.

                    MINDY
Here, Bonzo. (makes kissing sounds) Monkey wanna cracker?

                    MANDY
Don't let him grab it, draw him out.

                    MINDY
Monkey no wanna cracker? He no wanna.

                    MANDY
Beer nuts, Bomba?

                    ALAPETIA
He don't want nuts & crackers. Try the banana.

                    MANDY
Come on, Kong. You must be sick of this smelly old heiny you're stuck in.

                    MINDY
We gotta Chiquita for ya, Mr. Muggs.

                    MANDY
Yummy Yummy In the Tummy.

                    FARTS
He's crawling.

                    MANDY
He's reaching out.

                    RENE
Where are we, an AA meeting?

                              MANDY
Shut up.

                              MINDY
He wants the banana.

                              MANDY
Hmmm. Nice pink eyes. Long dark lashes.

                              MINDY
Quickly. Is there anyone in this crowd with a Big Thumb?

                           THE CROWD
I gotta Big Thumb.

                              MINDY
Show me quickly.

                                        Everyone displays their thumbs.
You. Commere.

                              MANDY
Come onnnnnnnn MONKEY! Come to Papa.

                              MINDY
When the monkey falls out, stick your thumb up Fart's ass, as fast as you can...
and keep it there.

                              MANDY
This is critical.

                              FARTS
I may shit as well as fart.

                              RENE
                                   (yells out
                                   and waves)
THANKS FOR SHARING!

                              MANDY
What a tail and schvantz this monkey's got.

                              MINDY
HERE SHE BLOWS.

                              MANDY
MY GOD! THE MOBY DICK OF MONKEY PENIS!

                              MINDY
PLUG HIM, THUMBS.

                                        The GUY WITH THE BIG THUMB
                                        plugs Fart's butt.

                              FARTS
I can't hold the gas no more.

                         MAN WITH BIG THUMB
My thumb's under considerable pressure here.

                         MINDY & MANDY
DON'T FART.

                            ALAPETIA
Hold on, baby, be brave. You can do it.

SCENE 13: BLACKOUTS FROM THE HAIRLESS HINEY... BANGKOK

THE MEAT LOCKER... BASEMENT OF THE
HAIRLESS HINEY

MADAME CHEW WEE, MISTRESS OF THE MEAT
ENTERS WITH HER BEST BOY, LEGS CHIJUAJUA

LEGS

WE IS OPEN FOR BUSINESS!

CHEWEE

No, Legs. Bad English. I is open for business, Okay?

LEGS

Gotcha, oh supple broad with sphincters of steel. I worship your bottomless Pit.

CHEWEE

Enough, already, with verbal foreplay. Bring me meat-seekers, that's my game.

LEGS
                              Yells offstage

BRING 'EM IN, FARTS!

                              FARTS LEVECQUE enters in full
                              regalia, farting all the way.

FARTS

First, I refuse to apologize for my condition.

CHEWEE

No apology necessary... everyone who works here knows about that.

FARTS

They turn away, leave the room, laugh... choke... gag. I suspect the help don't take me seriously...

CHEWEE

You can't predict what the "help" will do. Calm down. First customer please.

FARTS

I'm foul and full of farts,,, yes I am... Some say I fart to get attention. Look at me, honey... I don't need farts to get attention. Gotta look out for my health. My gramma told me, years back, never hold a fart when you can let it go. When you don't fart, that's when you worry. Grammy knew some geezer in Coral Gables, claimed he never farted in his life. Imagine the toxins! The fucker exploded in a supermarket. Not me, not Percy Levecque. No way. (HE FARTS GRANDLY)

FARTS (CONTINUES)
Madame Chewy, excuse me for holding the floor this way... I wanted you all to know I'm not ashamed... I'm Black, Proud and Noxious. (SMILES SWEETLY)

CHEWEE
I appreciate your candor. Can we go on now?

FARTS
Oh, yeah, sure. Just wanted to clear the air. Thanks for your patience and understanding. (after a deep sigh) Ahh... Now that I've purged myself of anxiety.... Enter Brenda & Brandon Troutwine.

BRANDON & BRENDA ENTER
nervous and excited, cross-dressed & dissolute.

CHEWEE
I am Madame Chewhee. Welcome to The Hairless Hiney's Fresh Meat Locker. You wish... ?

BRANDON
(in women's drag)
We were told "fresh meat" costs extra.

CHEWEE
Yeah. Fresh meat is always "extra" at the Hairless Hiney.

BRENDA
(in male drag &
mustache)
I told you, Brandon, we get the room, VCR, toys and tapes with the tour...

LEGS
(breaks in)
Everything else is more... much more.

BRANDON & BRENDA
(together)
Okay then... we want...

LEGS
Orders must be one at a time.

BRENDA
You go first, dear.

BRANDON
Thanks, mommy. I could go for a nice dead Lesbian right now.

                              BRENDA
Me, too!

                              CHEWEE
We'll see what we can do. MANDY?!

                              FARTS
MANDY!

                              LEGS
MANDY!

                                        MANDY enters from freezer
                                        covered with blood.

                              CHEWEE
Holy Christ!

                              MANDY
Are we open? Are we back in business?

                              CHEWEE
Change your frock.

                              MANDY
I was cutting loins for Roy Cohn's Bar Mitzvah.

                              CHEWEE
Later with the loins, already. Gotta dead Lesbian back there?

                              BRENDA
We need two.

                              BRANDON
A frilly one for me.

                              BRENDA
I'll take a body-builder with tits of tungsten.

                              CHEWEE
Hold it!

                              LEGS
Wait a minute!

CHEWEE

You prepared to pay the going price for dead Lesbians? You be picky-picky, gonna cost you plenty more.

BRANDON & BRENDA

How much more?

CHEWEE
(looks at price
chart)

Dead Lesbians on ice? 400 a piece.

BRANDON & BRENDA

$400!!??

LEGS

FOUR HUNDRED! You deaf, or what?

BRANDON

We can cover that, Brenda.

BRENDA

What about Bucky's braces?

BRANDON

I don't mind he looks like Bugs Bunny. Do you?

BRENDA

Not really. We can put it on the card. You take Visa?

CHEWEE

We take anything. Passports. Jewelry. You got gold?

LEGS

We take gold.

BRANDON

A frilly at 400 is a steal.

BRENDA

$400 for Miss Newark, right?

CHEWEE

I said 400 apiece for whatever's in the freezer. You be picky... two gees a pop.

LEGS

You got 4,000? We can get you what you want?

                              BRANDON
We could sell the Porsche.

                              BRENDA
I'd rather dump the condo in Aspen.

                              CHEWEE
MANDY?!

                              MANDY
Don't holler. I'm here.

                              CHEWEE
Have Mindy pop in the locker & drag me out some dead Lesbians. An
assortment if she's got 'em.

                              MANDY
MINDY? I'M COMING BACK FOR DEAD LESBIANS!

                                        MINDY enters, covered in blood.

                              MINDY
Why, now? Why Lesbians?

                              EVERYBODY
Why not?

                              MINDY
                       (officiously checks
                       her clipboard)
According to my inventory, which is seldom wrong, we have one dead Lesbian,
Madame Chewee.

                              BRANDON
                       (avidly)
Is she frilly?

                              MINDY
She's dead, undressed, in poor condition. If you want her, she's yours.

                              BRENDA
I was hoping for an aerobics instructor.

                              MINDY
The one we got is 82. Knockers to her knees. A rudimentary penis.

                              MANDY
Excuse me. My partner will now describe this penis, in detail. For myself, I'm
up to here with penis... I gotta fresh fairy needs freezing fast.

LEGS

So freeze the dead faggot already... send Bruno down to Labia's for Lesbians.

CHEWEE

Yes. When we say, "No reasonable request refused," we mean it. These folks are prepared to pay top dollar.

LEGS

Four thousand... special order.

BRANDON

Too much. We can't cover 4000.

BRENDA

You give discounts for good intentions?

LEGS

For the freshness alone, gonna cost you 4000.

BRANDON

We could sell Bucky.

BRENDA

Our son?

BRANDON

To be honest, I'm not all that fond of him.

BRENDA

Sure, he's a pain in the ass...

BRANDON

His mouth alone costs an arm and a leg.

BRENDA

Not his fault he was born with big teeth, hon...

BRANDON

As big as keys on grand pianos?

BRENDA

Enough to make Lionel Hampton green with envy.

BRANDON

Bucky's breath is no prize package either...

BRENDA

I'd rather kiss a St. Bernard goodnight.

                              BRANDON
Head the size of a casaba melon.

                              BRENDA
No ears.

                              BRANDON
Gotta nice butt...

                              BRENDA
And a fat schwantz.

                              BRANDON
Almost no brain at all.

                              BRENDA
We could say he wandered away from the hotel.

                              BRANDON
Vanished in the back alleys of Bangkok.

                              BRENDA
Fell in the Suey Canal and drowned.

                              BRANDON
We could get ourselves...

                              BRENDA
... A fresh, dead Lesbian...

                              BRANDON
Bucky could get laid, at last... and we'd have plenty left over for shopping.

                          BRANDON & BRENDA
Let's sell the pumpkin!

                              BRENDA
Excuse me, Madame Chewee?

                               LEGS
You come up with the gelt, schmucks?

                              BRANDON
We were wondering, would you take a live twelve-year-old boy in exchange for
one dead Lesbian?

                              CHEWEE
Young boys go for top dollar at The Hairless Hiney.

BRENDA

My hubby and I would be ever so grateful if you'd take the chubby little shit off
our hands...

BRANDON

Even steven.

CHEWEE

Can you produce this boy?

BRENDA

We did already. He's our son, Bucky.

BRANDON

At the hotel, chained to the sink.

CHEWEE

Your son?! You want to trade you son!?

BRENDA

We understand that's common practice in Southeast Asia.

SCENE 14: BILLY RELEASES HIS FATHER FROM BONDAGE

A private hospital on the Upper East Side.
Father in hospital whites. The last stages of
the taint. BILLY enters with flowers.

BILLY
(sings)

While tearing off
A game of golf
I may make a play for the caddy
But if I do
I don't follow through
Cause my heart belongs to Daddy

FATHER

Oh, Billy, is that you?

BILLY
(steps into the light)

Happy Father's Day, Dad.

FATHER

Been so long.

BILLY

Fifteen years.

FATHER

Gee, you grew up to look like me.

BILLY

The way you looked then, when I was little. You look more like Grandpa.

FATHER

I've been sick.

BILLY

You're positive.

FATHER

Who told you? Ruth?

BILLY

Mom and a couple of the old fags from Boy Love Inc.

FATHER

We had a lot of fun together, didn't we?

BILLY

You mean killing teenage boys?

FATHER

That was a tradition in our family, you know that. We had great sex, didn't we, you and me?

BILLY

You had me on so many drugs, all I remember is the pain, the disposal of the bodies, the smell of death in the house.

FATHER

Billy, please, I may never see you again in this world. Let's not talk about the bad stuff... Look, if you're gonna bring up the garage, the basement, hammer handles, and ice tongs again...

BILLY

You remember details very well.

FATHER

Why not? Those afternoons were the highlights of my life?

BILLY

Highlights! You raped me with a turkey baster. Bit me so hard on the back of my neck, took six stitches to close, tetanus shots for a month. Told Doc Connelley I was bitten by Rex.

FATHER

I was out of my mind.

BILLY

What are you now? Sane?

FATHER

I'm dying, Billy. All I'm asking for is a little understanding... forgiveness.

BILLY

You want me to forgive you?

FATHER

I cared about your body... I trained you... on the wrestling team, undefeated...

BILLY

You sucked all the feeling out of me, hurt me, then dumped me. 'Cause why? Tell me?

FATHER

I didn't dump you.

BILLY

I'd wait for you after that, every Saturday. I'd hang around behind the garage for
you, like a dog. All because you caught me in bed with Pete Stapp.

FATHER

You were ready then, I let you go.

BILLY

You kicked me out.

FATHER

You were a man.

BILLY

I was fifteen years old!

FATHER

I figured, hell, he don't get off with his old dad the way he used to... I let you go.
For years I hoped & prayed you'd come around, give me a buzz once in a while,
let me know what you're up to.

BILLY

No good. Does that satisfy your curiosity?

FATHER

I don't fear death, BIlly, I welcome it with open arms. But I want you to
terminate me, son, not the taint. You Billy, my sexy little boy.

BILLY

I'm not your "sexy boy," I'm your son!

FATHER

Don't give me that crap, Billy. You were sexy and you knew it when you were
eight. I never went after a kid didn't put the make on me first. Never.

BILLY

Bullshit!

FATHER

You can tell as young as 5 or 6 if a boy's gonna come on to you by his butt, does
it jut... pull the material up and tight at the crotch... with you always up on pop's
lap... grind your hard little buns against me, make me swell up watching Sabu,
the Elephant Boy.

BILLY

You made me sit on your lap.

FATHER

You wanted to make me stiff.

BILLY

Sabu made you hot. Latin boys turned you on. Why you took me to the tanning salon all winter, dyed my hair and eyebrows black, put forest green contacts in my eyes when i was nine. I still go through long periods of time, pretending I'm Latin.

FATHER

Everybody thought you looked great.

BILLY

You ruined me, my mom...

FATHER

Your mother went nutz on her own, no help from me.

BILLY

She got into drugs by you...

FATHER

Not by me. Her girlfriend, Lois.

BILLY

You drove her off the deep end.

FATHER

She drove herself.

BILLY

How many times did I come to dinner with blood on my hands? Or semen? Or both?

FATHER

I don't me-member that.

BILLY

You don't remember hanging around the house all weekend in a posing strap, covered in grease, smelling of sandalwood and grass, dumbbells stashed all over the fuckin' house? Mom opens the closet door, you're there in the dark doing preacher curls.

FATHER

I need my privacy too, you know. In war you reach for what remains through smoke and flame.

BILLY

What are you talking about?

FATHER

I'm beyond tears... past memory.

BILLY

Not me, dad. I remember everything. I couldn't take a shower in gym for all the scars & bites on my little boy's body from playing with Daddy, lifting weights with Daddy, wrestling with Daddy, dumping bodies with Daddy Daddy Daddy... Shit-sick American daddy... I should kill you for what you did to my head & heart, you sanctimonious 60's boy-fucker.

FATHER

I wanted to bury alive the madness in my loins, the ticking bomb that slaps against all mens' thighs. This is why men go to war! (grabs his cock) This switchblade knife of flesh where all hardness spends itself. Polluted cream our udders can't contain.

BILLY

Oh God, what terrible crimes of sex & death you've wrought upon my life, pop. This madness that you've made, you made for naught.

FATHER

I only sought to murder thought and put an end to guilt. That was my father's gift to me. O the world he gave us all Boy Love Inc.
A dinka dee
A dinka doo,
A dinka dee
Oh, what a nite
For nightmares

BILLY

You told me one's own death is all we're born to mourn. The end of others matters little, if at all. Easily achieved and soon forgotten.

FATHER

I thought I'd never die. Never entered my mind.

BILLY

Do you believe in death now? Now that death has come to make you stop, do you believe in death?

FATHER

I do, as long as you're the one who does the deed. Put me to sleep forever. Kiss me, Billy. Kill me.

BILLY

No, Pop. I've spent the last 15 years atoning for my childhood, trying to reclaim what's left of me... I have no lovers or friends. My friends are books. My lovers? The memories of all the boys we killed & dumped on the Jersey Shore. I work in a toll booth. Spend my free time in the library. Go to church every Sunday. Pray for God to forgive me, that I might sleep without the terrible thoughts tearing at me when I close my eyes at night. I won't kill you, dad. The life your father trained you to embrace; the tradition of wasting & destroying that created Boy Love Inc. ends here, with us. We're the last of an unholy line. I will never see your face again. When I walk out of this room, I won't look back. The rest is silence.

FATHER

Where will you go?

BILLY

I don't know. To the police or the river. I pray your death is slow, that you smother at the end in the faces & bodies of all the beautiful young men you murdered. And God help me, I love you still.

FATHER

Oh Billy, won't you kiss me once before we drift apart?

BILLY

You look sixteen, pop. So sick, so young. Can see you now as you must have been in Red Bank as a boy. HOt young kid. Humpy body. No hope. Kiss me.

(They do.)

Welcome home.

BILLY exits. Climbs the stairway. Does not look back.

BLACKOUT

PUFF THE MAGIC DRAGON

Made in the USA
Middletown, DE
01 August 2022

70298341R00077